John Yates Beall

Trial of John Y. Beall

As a spy and guerrillero, by Military Commission. Vol. 1

John Yates Beall

Trial of John Y. Beall
As a spy and guerrillero, by Military Commission. Vol. 1

ISBN/EAN: 9783337297749

Printed in Europe, USA, Canada, Australia, Japan

Cover: Foto ©ninafisch / pixelio.de

More available books at **www.hansebooks.com**

TRIAL

OF

JOHN Y. BEALL,

AS A

SPY AND GUERRILLERO,

BY MILITARY COMMISSION.

NEW YORK:
D. APPLETON AND COMPANY,
443 & 445 BROADWAY.
1865.

PROCEEDINGS

IN THE

CASE OF JOHN Y. BEALL.

Special Orders }
No. 14. }   Headquarters Department of the East, }
                            New York City, *Jan.* 17*th*, 1865. }

6. A Military Commission, to consist of the following named officers, will assemble at Fort Lafayette, N. Y. H., at 11 A.M., on Friday, January 20th, 1865, or as soon thereafter as practicable, for the trial of such cases as may be brought before it, by orders from these Headquarters, to sit without regard to hours, and to hold its sessions in New York City, if the convenience of the service require it; four members to constitute a quorum, for the transaction of business.

Detail for the Court.

Brig. General Fitz Henry Warren, U. S. V.
    "   W. H. Morris, U. S. V.
Colonel M. S. Howe, 3d U. S. Cav.
    "   H. Day, U. S. A.
Brev. Lieut. Col. R. F. O'Bierne, 14th U. S. Infantry.
Major G. W. Wallace, 6th U. S. Infantry.
Major John A. Bolles, A. D. C., is appointed Judge Advocate.

                                       By command of Major Gen. Dix.
                                               D. T. Van Buren,
                                                       Assistant Adjutant General.

Fort Lafayette, New York Harbor,
11 o'clock A.M., Friday, *Jan.* 20*th*, 1865.

The Commission constituted and convened by the foregoing order, met in obedience thereto.

Present, all the members, namely:

    Brig. General FITZ HENRY WARREN, U. S. V.
    "   W. H. MORRIS, U. S. V.
    Colonel M. S. HOWE, 3d U. S. Cav.
    Colonel H. DAY, U. S. Army.
    Brev. Lieut. Col. R. F. O'BIERNE, 14th U. S. Infantry.
    Major G. W. WALLACE, 6th U. S. Infantry.

Present, also, the Judge Advocate, and JOHN Y. BEALL, the accused, who was brought in for trial.

The foregoing order was read aloud in presence and hearing of the accused; and he being asked if he objected to any member named in the detail, answered that he did not, but that he desired to protest against being tried by any Military Commission.

In presence and hearing of the accused, the Commission was then duly sworn by the Judge Advocate, the Judge Advocate by the President, and JAMES E. MUNSON as Stenographer and Clerk to the Commission, by the Judge Advocate.

The Judge Advocate inquired of the accused if he was ready to proceed to trial, and he answered that he was not, but desired time to procure counsel and prepare for his defence. At his request the Commission granted him until 11 o'clock A.M., Wednesday, January 25th, and the trial was postponed accordingly.

The Commission then adjourned to meet to-morrow, January 21st, at the Department Headquarters, New York City, at 12 o'clock M., for the purpose of commencing the trial of Harris Hoyt.

                    JOHN A. BOLLES, Maj. and A. D. C.,
                                    Judge Advocate.

Fort Lafayette, New York Harbor,
11 o'clock A.M., Wednesday, *Jan.* 25*th*, 1865.

The Commission met pursuant to adjournment. Present, all the members.

Present, also, the Judge Advocate, and the accused, John Y. Beall, who was brought in for trial.

The record of the proceedings of January 20th was read by the Judge Advocate, and approved.

The Judge Advocate asked the accused if he was ready to proceed to trial, to which the accused answered that he had written for counsel; that he had handed the letter to Colonel Burke, but had received no answer.

The Judge Advocate said that the letter referred to by the accused was delivered to him on the 20th of January, by Colonel Burke; that he carried it that day to Mr. Brady's Office, it being addressed to that gentleman; that Mr. Brady being out, he handed it to Mr. Traphagen, who said that if it was possible Mr. Brady would attend to the case; if not, Mr. Brady or he (Mr. Traphagen) would endeavor to procure competent counsel to come down and consult with Capt. Beall; and he then wrote a pass for Mr. Brady, or any other member of the bar, to visit the fort at any and all times, as counsel for Capt. Beall, and that he had this morning received the following note from Mr. Brady:

January 23, 1865.

Major JOHN A. BOLLES,

MY DEAR SIR:—I am very much obliged to you for your courtesy and consideration in regard to the case at Fort Lafayette. Unfortunately the trial I have in the Superior Court has commenced, and I must attend to it from day to day. I have sought to procure other counsel for Mr. Beall, but cannot at present obtain any whom I can in all respects commend. I trust it may not be inconsistent with the public interest to postpone the trial at Fort Lafayette for a week. I send this by my friend William H. Ryan, Esq.

Yours truly,

JAMES T. BRADY.

Mr. Ryan being present, the Commission inquired of him if Mr. Brady would be able to be present and act as counsel for the accused, in case the trial were adjourned for one week; and Mr. Ryan answered that he would.

The Judge Advocate exhibited to the accused three letters which purported to come from him, and which were addressed to persons in Toronto, Canada West, and in Richmond, Va., and informed the accused that, if he would reduce to writing in the form of an affidavit a statement of the facts he expected to prove by the persons or documents named in those letters, he should probably admit that the witnesses or documents, if presented in Court, would so say, and thus save the Government the delay, and the accused the trouble and expense of getting them here.

The accused stated that he wrote the letters, and that he would prepare the statement suggested, and so far as Mr. Brady was concerned, would be ready for trial on Wednesday, February 1st.

On motion of a member of the Commission, the application of the accused for delay was granted, and the trial was postponed until Wednesday at 11 o'clock A.M., February 1st, 1865, with the understanding that at that time the trial should proceed.

The Commission then adjourned until to-morrow, January 26th, at 12 o'clock M., to meet at Department Headquarters for the transaction of other business.

JOHN A. BOLLES, Major and A.D.C.,
Judge Advocate.

Fort Lafayette, New York Harbor,
11 o'clock A.M., Wednesday, *Feb. 1st*, 1865.

The Commission met pursuant to adjournment.

Present all the members.

Present, also, the Judge Advocate, and the accused John Y. Beall, who was brought in for trial.

By leave of the Commission James T. Brady, Esq., appeared as counsel for the accused.

The Judge Advocate inquired of the accused if he was ready to plead to the charges and specifications, and the accused answered that he was.

The accused was then arraigned on the following charges and specifications, which were read aloud in his presence and hearing, and to which after they were so read the accused pleaded that he was not guilty.

CHARGES AND SPECIFICATIONS AGAINST JOHN Y. BEALL

CHARGE 1st. *Violation of the laws of war.*

Specification 1. In this that John Y. Beall, a citizen of the insurgent State of Virginia, did on or about the 19th day of September, 1864, at or near Kelly's Island, in the State of Ohio, without lawful authority, and by force of arms, seize and capture the Steamboat *Philo Parsons.*

Specification 2. In this that John Y. Beall, a citizen of the insurgent State of Virginia, did on or about the 19th day of September, 1864, at or near Middle Bass Island, in the State of Ohio, without lawful authority, and by force of arms, seize, capture, and sink the Steamboat *Island Queen*.

Specification 3. In this that John Y. Beall, a citizen of the insurgent State of Virginia, was found acting as a spy at or near Kelly's Island, in the State of Ohio, on or about the 19th day of September, 1864.

Specification 4. In this that John Y. Beall, a citizen of the insurgent State of Virginia, was found acting as a spy on or about the 19th day of September, 1864, at or near Middle Bass Island, in the State of Ohio.

Specification 5. In this that John Y. Beall, a citizen of the insurgent State of Virginia, was found acting as a spy on or about the 16th day of December, 1864, at or near Suspension Bridge in the State of New York.

Specification 6. In this that John Y. Beall, a citizen of the insurgent State of Virginia, being without lawful authority, and for unlawful purposes, in the State of New York, did in said State of New York undertake to carry on irregular and unlawful warfare as a guerrilla; and in the execution of said undertaking, attempted to destroy the lives and property of the peaceable and unoffending inhabitants of said State, and of persons therein travelling, by throwing a train of cars and the passengers in said cars from the railroad track, on the railroad between Dunkirk and Buffalo, by placing obstructions across said track; all this in said State of New York, and on or about the 15th day of December, 1864, at or near Buffalo.

CHARGE 2d. *Acting as a Spy.*

Specification 1. In this that John Y. Beall, a citizen of the insurgent State of Virginia, was found acting as a spy in the State of Ohio, at or near Kelly's Island, on or about the 19th day of September, 1864.

Specification 2. In this that John Y. Beall, a citizen of the insurgent State of Virginia, was found acting as a spy in the State of Ohio, on or about the 19th day of September, 1864, at or near Middle Bass Island.

Specification 3. In this that John Y. Beall, a citizen of the insurgent State of Virginia, was found acting as a spy in the State of New York, at or near Suspension Bridge, on or about the 16th day of September, 1864.

JOHN A. BOLLES, Major and A.D.C.,
Judge Advocate.

NEW YORK, 17*th January*, 1865.

Headquarters Department of the East, }
New York City, *January* 17*th*, 1865.

The above-named Beall will be brought for trial before the Military Commission of which Brig. Gen. F. H. Warren is President.

JOHN A. DIX,
Major General.

To these charges and specifications the accused pleaded not guilty, and thereupon the Judge Advocate called WALTER O. ASHLEY, a witness for the prosecution, who, being duly sworn, in presence of the accused, testified as follows:—

Question by Judge Advocate. State your name, place of residence, and occupation?

Answer. My name is WALTER O. ASHLEY. I am clerk and part owner of the steamboat *Philo Parsons;* residence, City of Detroit, State of Michigan.

Q. Look at the accused; have you ever seen him before?

A. I have. On the 19th day of September last I saw him the first time.

Q. State the circumstances under which you saw him. State the transactions which brought you first into company with the accused, beginning on the 18th of September.

A. On Sunday, the 18th of September, about six o'clock in the evening, I was on board the steamboat *Philo Parsons,* in the cabin alone, at the boat's dock in Detroit; she being a boat sailing from Detroit to the City of Sandusky, touching regularly at the Canadian port of Amherstburgh, and occasionally at Sandwich. On the evening of Sunday, Mr. Bennett G. Burley came aboard the boat, and inquired for Ashley. I told him my name was Ashley. He then said he intended to go down as a passenger, in the morning, to Sandusky; that three friends were going with him; and he requested that the boat would stop at Sandwich, a small town on the Canada side of the river below Detroit, and take on those three friends as passengers. I remarked that it was not customary for the boat to stop at Sandwich. He then asked it as a personal favor that the boat would stop and take on his friends. I then agreed, providing he, Burley, would take the boat himself at Detroit, and let me know for sure that his friends would be ready to come on board at Sandwich, that the boat would call for them. He then went away. The next morning, being Monday the 19th of September, the boat left Detroit at eight o'clock in the morning, with freight and passengers. As the boat was swinging away from the dock, Burley came to me and reminded me of my promise to stop the boat at

Sandwich. At the time the boat left Detroit, Capt. S. F. Atwood was in command of her, but he stepped off at Middle Bass Island, where he resides. I told Capt. Atwood that the boat would have to stop at Sandwich, and he stopped and took these three friends of Burley at Sandwich.

Q. Who were they?

A. The accused was one, and there were two others.

Q. Coming on board, did they report their names?

A. They did not. I did not record the names; it has been my custom sometimes to record passengers' names on long routes, but I did not on this.

Q. What was the dress of the accused when he came on board, civil or military?

A. They were all dressed in citizens' clothes, the entire party; they had no baggage; they were very gentlemanly in their appearance; they said they were taking a little pleasure trip—might stop perhaps at Kelly's Island; did not know exactly where they would go; paid their fare to Sandusky. The fare is the same to Kelly's Island as it is to Sandusky. The boat then proceeded to Malden, Canada West, about fifteen miles further down the river; about twenty-five men came on board there at Malden, and they all paid their fare also; that port is the same as Amherstburgh; all the baggage brought on board by the party was a very old trunk tied up with cord, a rope tied around it. It was taken in at the after gangway of the boat by two of the roughest looking subjects in the party; most of the party were roughly dressed in citizens' dress.

Q. If the contents of that trunk became afterwards known, state what they were.

A. It afterwards became known, and it contained revolvers and hatchets.

Q. Leaving Amherstburgh, where did you go?

A. The boat proceeded on its way to Sandusky. Every thing passed off quietly during the day. It was about half-past nine in the morning when we left Amherstburgh. Every thing passed off quietly until about four o'clock in the afternoon. The boat stopped at a number of islands transacting business and taking on passengers. At four o'clock in the afternoon she had just left Kelly's Island. She was two miles from Kelly's Island. Kelly's Island is in the State of Ohio, six miles from the American shore on Lake Erie. In sailing from Kelly's Island to Sandusky we sail nearly south; we were about two miles I should judge from Kelly's Island toward the American shore, and some four miles off the Ohio main shore.

Q. State what then occurred.

A. I was standing on the main deck of the boat; Captain Atwood was ashore.

Q. Who was in charge of the boat?

A. I was in charge of the business of the boat; I am not a sailor; the mate was sailing the boat; he was sailing master in charge of the sailing of the boat, and I was in charge of the affairs of the boat. As I said before, I was standing on the main deck in front of the office and the ladies' cabin; the passengers at this time—there were about eighty, nearly half of whom were ladies—were in the upper cabin. Three men came up to me, drew revolvers and levelled them, and said if I offered any resistance they would shoot me.

Q. Who were the men?

A. They were three of the party; the accused was not one of those three, neither was Mr. Burley at this time. Bennett G. Burley came from the forward part of the boat aft, followed by fifteen or twenty. Burley had a revolver in his hand and levelled it at me and said, "Get into that cabin," meaning the ladies' cabin, "or you are a dead man." The parties that followed him were not armed at this time. He commenced counting, "one, two, three," at the same time. He had not counted a great many, probably, before I was inside the door; two men were stationed outside of the door. I stayed inside of the door, and they were stationed outside the door, for the purpose of keeping me in the cabin, I suppose. One stood one side of the door, and the other the other, with revolvers in their hands; the party gathered around this old trunk I spoke of before; the cords were cut, the lid taken off, and they armed themselves from that with revolvers and hatchets; most of them had two large revolvers, and a portion of them hatchets; they then took forcible possession of the boat, and made prisoners of all on board. I was kept in the cabin for about one hour. I could look out through the door on the main deck and see every thing that was going on. Bennett G. Burley had charge of this deck at the time. Burley with an axe which he found on board smashed the baggage room door open—I don't know for what purpose—then went forward and smashed the saloon door; he then went with the axe, smashed the trotting sulky to pieces, which was thrown overboard; he then with the men under him commenced to throw the freight overboard, consisting of household goods, tobacco and iron; the iron was thrown overboard first. I won't say that I saw the household goods thrown overboard; the iron was thrown overboard, perhaps the household goods were not; about an hour I should judge after the capture of the boat, the accused, Capt. Beall, came to me and asked me if I was in charge of the office. I told him I was. He then asked me if I was in charge of the boat's papers. I told him I was. He then said he was in charge of the party, and wanted the boat's papers, and I went into the office and gave him the papers, and he took them and carried them away.

Q. At the time he asked you for the papers did he make any statement to you as to who or what he was, or what his purpose was?

A. He did not say directly. I made a request that he would not destroy the steamboat. He did not say directly whether he should destroy the boat or should not. He said something to the effect that if I was a United States soldier, or United States officer, and had seized any of *their* vessels, or something to that effect—I won't say the exact words—that I would probably destroy the vessel. He did not say to me that he was a Confederate States officer—some of the others did say so; said the party were Confederate States soldiers, and that the expedition was in charge of Confederate States officers. Directly after the capture of the boat she was headed down the lake; not towards Sandusky; directly off from her course for Sandusky. She ran down the lake for half an hour, I should judge, and then turned around and ran up the lake to Middle Bass Island for the purpose of wooding, and also for the purpose of putting the passengers ashore.

Q. She ran to Middle Bass Island and there *did* wood, and there the passengers *were* put on shore?

A. Yes, sir. Middle Bass Island is in the State of Ohio, about ten miles from the shore. She had been lying there about fifteen minutes when the steamboat *Island Queen* came alongside of the boat; she is a steamboat that runs from Sandusky to these islands with freight and passengers both, making the round trip every day. She came alongside of the *Philo Parsons* and made fast alongside. The party that were then in charge of the *Philo Parsons* went aboard the *Island Queen*, seized her, made prisoners of all on board, and brought them all on board of the *Philo Parsons* as prisoners; part of them were put in the cabin of the *Philo Parsons*, and part of them were put into the hold. The passengers of both boats were afterwards all put ashore on Middle Bass Island. When the boat had been lying at this island I should judge about an hour—I was in my office, I was allowed to go there; there were two ladies and a gentleman in the office—Captain Beall came to the door and said: "Ladies you will have to go ashore now, as we are agoing to use this boat." He gave the young man permission to go also. They started out and I followed them; I went back for the purpose of picking up my books and papers; Capt. Beall came back and Burley with him; I stood at my desk with Capt. Beall at one side, and Mr. Burley on the other; I asked if they were going to put me ashore; they said they were going to allow me to go ashore;

I asked permission to take the boat's books; Capt. Beall said I should not take them, that I should not take any thing belonging to the boat; I then said I had some private promissory notes in an envelope and requested leave to take them; Burley said: "Let me see them." I produced them; he looked at them, said he "could not collect them," and gave them to me. Capt. Beall then said: "We want your money." I opened the money drawer, in which there was very little money, perhaps eight or ten dollars; they took that out. Burley then said: "You have more money; let us have it." I put my hand into my vest pocket and took out a roll of bills of about $100, and laid it on the desk; I then requested again that I might be allowed to take the books, but they refused to let me take them; I was then put ashore.

Q. If you saw what became of that roll of bills, state what was done with it.

A. The roll of bills was taken between them; Capt. Beall and Burley took the roll of bills, and also took the money out of the drawer; they took it between them; they both made a demand for the money; Capt. Beall made the demand first, and Mr. Burley afterwards made the demand.

Q. Which of the two took the roll of bills after you laid it on the desk?

A. They took it between them; I will not swear which one positively, they took it between them; they both made the demand; they said, "Give us the money;" I then went on shore.

Q. After you went on shore state what you observed was done with either or both of the boats—the boats I understand both remained in the possession of the seizing party?

A. Yes, sir. After I went on shore and had been on shore about half an hour, the boats were started in the direction of Sandusky; they were alongside lashed together. It was a moonlight night, and when about two or three miles out I noticed the *Island Queen* drifting from the *Philo Parsons*; it afterwards proved that she was scuttled; she drifted about four miles, and drifted on to a reef and was afterwards raised; she was nearly full of water when she was raised.

Q. Are you able from your own inspection to state that she was, and how she was scuttled?

A. Not from my own observation.

Q. You state from your own observation that you saw her drifting?

A. Yes, sir.

Q. How much else can you state from your own observation as to what became of her?

A. I can state that I saw her the next morning on my way to

Sandusky, on what is called Chickenolee Reef; there was nine feet of water on the reef; she drew about four feet of water, and she was sunk on the reef where the water was about nine feet deep.

Q. How far was that from the point where you saw her drifting the evening before?

A. About five miles.

Q. When and where did you next see the accused?

A. I next saw the accused in the city of New York after his arrest.

Q. Have you stated all that passed between you and him on board the *Philo Parsons* on the 19th of September?

A. I think I have stated every thing that would be of any account; I saw him considerably.

The Judge Advocate said he had no further questions to ask the witness.

Cross-examination by Accused.

Q. How long were you clerk of the *Philo Parsons*?

A. Two seasons; it was my second season.

Q. What was your occupation before that?

A. I have been clerk on steamboats about nine years; clerk and part owner.

Q. In what other boats

A. The steamboat *Dot*, a steamboat that ran from Detroit to Port Huron, as a freight and passenger boat.

Q. Have you had any other occupation at any other time previous to that?

A. Previous to that I was clerk in stores from the time I was 13 or 14 until about the time I was 20.

Q. Have you now stated all the occupations you have had at any time in your life?

A. Previous to my going into a store which I think was when I was about 14—I might have been 15, I cannot tell exactly now—I was attending school; I was also with my uncle assisting him as clerk in a Post-Office; that is all, I think.

Q. Had you ever seen Burley or Beall before they came on board the *Philo Parsons* as you have stated?

A. I have no recollection of ever seeing them before, either of them; I saw Burley the 18th of September and Beall the 19th; I have no recollection of seeing either of them previous to that to know them.

Q. When the twenty-five persons came on board at Sandwich, which of them was it that made the remark about the pleasure-trip?

A. The twenty-five did not come on board at Sandwich, and the remark was made about the pleasure-trip when the three came on at Sandwich; Burley was the man who had something to say about that; I had more acquaintance with Burley than any of the rest of them; he was spokesman for the whole party; the other three I don't remember; Burley had something to say about the pleasure-trip the night before on Sunday.

Q. Was Beall present at the time when Burley made the observation?

A. I cannot say whether he was or not; I did not pay any particular attention to Beall until after the capture of the boat; I don't remember that he was present.

Q. Did Burley in any of these conversations with you state that he was a Confederate State officer; what his rank was?

A. No, sir; he said nothing on that subject at any time to me.

Q. You said that some of them did say that they were in the Confederate State service?

A. Yes, sir. The two men that were guarding me directly after the capture of the boat that stood outside of the door; I asked them what they intended to do, they said that they were Confederate State officers and soldiers, and that they intended to capture the United States steamer *Michigan*, and release their friends on Johnson's Island; and others said the same thing.

Q. You say that Burley was the spokesman of the party. Did he give all the orders that were executed in regard to the boat by the persons with him?

A. I saw more of Burley for the first two hours after the capture of the boat than of the accused; I did not see the accused for an hour or an hour and a half; I had supposed that Burley was in charge of the whole party, and in fact I supposed he was until Captain Beall came to me and requested me to give him the papers; he then said he was in charge of them; I supposed that Burley was in charge of the party up to that time.

Q. Give as nearly as you can what was the language of Beall when he made the announcement to you that he was in charge of the party.

A. He asked me if I was in charge of the office; I told him I was; he then asked if I was in charge of the boat's papers, and I told him I was; he said, "I am in charge of this party, and I want the boat's papers." I went into the office and gave them to him; I then said to him that I was part owner of the boat, and I hoped he would not destroy the boat. He said something to the effect that if I was a United States officer—I will give you the words as nearly as I can—that if I was a United States officer and had seized one of their vessels, that I would probably destroy it. He did not say that he should destroy the boat.

Q. Was the language he used this: "If you were a United States officer and had seized one of our boats, you would probably destroy it?"

A. Yes, sir. "Our boats," that is the language.

Q. Did he use any language to indicate what he meant by "our"?

A. No, sir, nothing but that.

Q. Up to this time had any one stated in Beall's presence that this was a party of Confederates?

A. Not in my hearing; as I said before I saw but very little of Captain Beall for an hour and a half or two hours after the capture of the boat.

Q. You have stated that revolvers were presented at you. Did any person actually make an attempt upon your life?

A. There were no shots fired; they were presented at me, and they said if I offered any resistance they would shoot me.

Q. Did Beall at any time or in any way interfere with you personally, either to threaten your life or to save it?

A. At the time the money was taken from me they had revolvers with them. I won't say that the revolvers were pointed at me.

Q. Are you sure that you saw Beall have a revolver at the time he was in the office when the money was delivered?

A. I am, sir.

Q. Have you a sufficient recollection of the weapon to describe it?

A. I have not, any further than that it was a revolver; it had the appearance of being a revolver.

Q. Are you acquainted with the different kinds of revolvers, so as to identify it in any way?

A. No, sir, I could not identify that revolver.

Q. Did Burley threaten to shoot you?

A. He did, sir.

Q. For what?

A. At the time of the capture of the boat, before they had made the general seizure of the boat, and made prisoners of all on board, he drew his revolver and told me to get into that cabin—meaning the ladies' cabin—or he would shoot me.

Q. At no other time?

A. No, sir, I think not.

Q. Did not Burley ask you for the key of the room where the baggage was kept, previous to smashing the door in; and did you not refuse, and say you had not the key?

A. I have not thought any thing in regard to that; just after I had stepped inside the door I heard some one, whether it was Burley or not I cannot say, call for the key. Burley said, ' I will make a key." He found an axe on board and smashed the door open; some one called for the key; I was not asked for the key; I do remember now, I heard some one call for the key to the baggage-room, and I remember Burley taking an axe and smashing the door in.

Q. Did Burley at any time threaten to shoot you because you did not deliver the key to him, or did not obey his orders, or comply with some request that he made?

A. The only time he threatened to shoot me was before the general seizure of the boat, as I stated; I think that was the only time.

Q. Did any person make such a threat to you other than Burley?

A. Three others that I spoke of in the first place, just previous to Burley making the threat.

Q. Was Beall present on either of those occasions?

A. No, sir; I did not see Beall for an hour or an hour and a half after the capture of the boat.

Q. Did you see him before the trunk was opened?

A. Not that I know of; as I said before, I have no recollection of seeing him until the time he made the demand for the boat's papers.

Q. Was there any occasion while Beall was in your presence that any person either threatened or made a movement, as if to shoot you, Beall interfering and preventing it?

A. I don't recollect of any thing of the kind.

Q. Did any such circumstance as this happen, that you being asked for the key, and either refusing or hesitating to give it up, a pistol was presented at you, and the threat made to shoot, and Beall remarked, " Don't kill him, I will make a key myself," or any thing of that character.

A. I don't recollect of any thing of that kind. It is possible that I might have seen Captain Beall, the accused, before the time that I allude to that he took the boat's papers, but I have no recollection of seeing him after the seizure of the boat, until that time.

Q. You say he was in citizen's dress like the other two persons who came on board?

A. Yes, sir.

Q. Had he a hat or cap on?

A. I won't swear positively. I don't pay very close attention to people's clothing.

Q. Was there any thing peculiar about any part of his dress that you observed?

A. No, sir, nothing peculiar.

Q. Did you hear any conversation between Beall and Burley, or Beall and any other person, in which they spoke of their design except what you have already stated to the Court?

A. No, sir.

Q. Had the small sum of money which was in the drawer been collected from the passengers?

A. The whole of it had been collected from passengers, or in payment of freight.

Q. Was there any money collected from any person, as if they were passengers, after the party took possession of the boat?

A. No, sir, not to my knowledge; I collected none.

Q. Can you now state what you have not answered specifically to the question put by the prosecution, which of these two persons it was that actually took into his hand the money that you produced?

A. I can swear that Captain Beall took some of it.

Q. As to the hundred dollars in the roll, I mean?

A. They both of them made the demand, and I laid the money on the desk.

Q. Who took it up?

A. The money was taken between them; I am not going to swear positively; I took the money out of the drawer; they both made the demand for the money.

Q. When Captain Beall asked you for the papers, as you say, did he say any thing about wanting such papers as showed the nationality of the steamboat?

A. I think he did; he asked for the boat's papers; I asked him if he wished the enrollment and license, he said he did; something to show what kind of boat she was, or something to that effect; that she was a United States vessel; and I produced the enrollment and license, and I stood by in the office when he read them; he read them in my presence, or a portion of them.

Q. Did he state any reason why he wanted the papers?

A. No further than he said he was in charge of the party and wished the papers.

Q. When he asked you for the money, or when the money was demanded, were you asked if you had any public money in your possession, or money that belonged to the United States?

A. I don't recollect that those words were used at all.

Q. Did any one of them designate the money asked for as money belonging to the boat?

A. Capt. Beall said in the first place: "We want your money;" and Burley said: "You have more money, and let us have it."

Q. Did either of them in any way designate or specify what money they were asking for, whether it was the money belonging to the boat, or all the money in your possession?

A. I think they did not designate. All the money I had, however, was the property of the boat, of myself and others interested in the boat.

Q. Did either of them say any thing to the effect that they did not want any private money that belonged to you personally?

A. No sir, they did not, not to my knowledge; the word private or personal I don't think was used; they gave me my personal papers—some personal notes; I did not claim any of the money as personal; I I claimed the notes as personal, that was all I claimed as personal.

Q. Did they take any papers except such as belonged to the boat?

A. No, Sir. I made a demand for these notes as my personal papers, and they gave them up.

Q. When the *Island Queen* attached herself to the *Philo Parsons*, were there any soldiers on the *Island Queen*?

A. There were about twenty or twenty-five unarmed United States soldiers going to Toledo to be mustered out of the service; they were in uniform.

Q. What became of them?

A. They were taken as prisoners, with the rest of the passengers, and were put into the hold with the rest of the passengers.

Q. What was the last you saw of them?

A. I was in the office; they were put ashore before I was; they were put ashore at Middle Bass Island, the place where I was put ashore.

Q. Where did you see Mr. Beall when you saw him in New York as you state?

A. I saw him at the Police Station in the City of New York?

Q. Who took you to see him?

A. I was taken by Col. Ludlow.

Q. Was he alone when you saw him?

A. No, sir; there were about twenty-five or thirty in the room with him.

Q. Had he a hat or cap on then?

A. I don't think he had any thing on at that time; I think not.

Q. Were you asked to point him out?

A. No, sir.

Q. Did you speak to him?

A. I did not at that time.

Q. Did he wear his hair and beard as he does now, when you saw him in New York?

A. The same as it is *now?* yes sir.

Q. How was it when you first saw him?

A. He had a moustache without whiskers.

The Accused said he had no further questions to ask the witness.

Examination by the Commission.

Q. State whether there was any military or naval mark or badge on the accused while he was on board the *Philo Parsons*.

A. There was not; they were dressed as citizens, in citizens' dress, and paid their fare as passengers, and were treated as passengers.

Q. Did Burley and Beall divide the money in any way, which you took and laid in a roll of bills on the desk?

A. They were taking the money when I left; I laid it on the desk, and they were taking the money; they both made the demand, and were both taking the money between them. I saw them taking the money between them and dividing it. I don't know any thing about how much either one of them took; there was an actual division of the money, and I saw it.

Re-examination by Judge Advocate.

Q. At the time the boat was captured, how far was she from Johnson's Island?

A. Johnson's Island is in Sandusky Bay, inside of the main shore. I should judge the boat was captured about six miles from Johnson's Island.

Q. How far is Kelly's Island from Johnson's Island?

A. About eight miles.

Q. How far is it from Middle Bass Island to Johnson's Island?

A. I should say thirteen or fourteen miles.

Q. Have you ever seen the United States war steamer *Michigan*?

A. I have seen her, but I never have been on board of her.

Q. Do you know where she was at the time of this affair?

A. She was lying off of Johnson's Island, I should say about a mile. I stated that I had never been on board the steamer *Michigan*. I was on board her six or seven years ago. I have not been since the war.

Re-cross-examination by Accused.

Q. You said the soldiers on board the *Island Queen* were unarmed?

A. Yes, sir.

Q. Do you know whether there were any arms on board of this vessel?

A. There were not; not to my knowledge.

Q. Did you examine to see whether there were or not?

A. I did not examine.

Q. During any part of the time you were on board after the capture of the *Philo Parsons*, was any flag displayed by this party?

A. Not while I was on board.

Q. Did not they display a flag afterwards to your knowledge?
A. Not to my recollection.

No further questions were asked; his testimony being read to the witness, he affirmed the same.

The Judge Advocate then called WILLIAM WESTON, a witness for the prosecution, who being duly sworn, in presence of the accused, testified as follows:

Examined by Judge Advocate.

Q. State your name, place of residence, and occupation.
A. WILLIAM WESTON, Sandusky City, Ohio. I have been fireman for the last five years.
Q. Have you ever seen the accused, Capt. Beall, before?
A. Yes, sir.
Q. When for the first time, and where?
A. The first time I saw him was on board the *Philo Parsons*, on the 19th of last September.
Q. State what you saw him do, and what you heard him say.
A. After the capture of the boat, and we got a little excited, he came forward, and told us what they were going to do with us, and the boat; I was a passenger on board; he said they were not going to hurt or harm any of us, and that they would land us as soon as they thought fit; he also stated that he was an escaped rebel prisoner from Johnson's Island, and that they had taken the boat for the purpose of capturing the United States vessel *Michigan*; he said they were going to liberate the prisoners on Johnson's Island, and were going to destroy the commerce on the Lakes; that is all I recollect he said.
Q. Did you see what was done with any of the freight on board the *Philo Parsons* after the boat was seized?
A. I did not see them do any thing with the freight, only they threw out one of my boxes, that I got afterwards on the beach, that was pitched out; that was after they landed us on the Island; they pitched one of my boxes into the water.
Q. Will you state whether Beall, the accused, had any arms about him or not, while on board the *Philo Parsons*.
A. I could not state; I did not see.
Q. How was he dressed?
A. He was dressed in citizens' clothes.
Q. Do you remember whether he wore a cap or a hat?
A. He wore a kind of a low-sized hat; a low-crowned hat.
Q. Where did you next see him after you were landed?

A. I did not see him after I was landed on the Island until I saw him here, at Fort Lafayette, when I was brought down to the fort to identify him.

Q. Did you hear on board the *Philo Parsons*, from himself or others, what was the name of the accused; what they called him?

A. Captain Beall.

Q. You heard him called Captain Beall?

A. I could not say whether he was the person or not; I heard somebody called Captain Beall.

Q. Can you state who appeared to be in command, or charge of the party who seized the *Philo Parsons?*

A. I could not state.

The Judge Advocate said he had no further questions to ask the witness.

Cross-examined by the Accused.

Q. When you were brought down to Fort Lafayette to point out Captain Beall, did you point out this man?

A. Yes, sir, when I saw him.

Q. Who was with him?

A. I could not state who was with him; I am a stranger, I don't know any of the men around.

Q. Didn't you point out another and a different man, who proved to be a man named Smedley?

A. No, sir.

Q. What was the first you saw of this person; who told you he was a rebel prisoner; where was he?

A. He came forward stating what they were going to do with us; that was the first time I saw him.

Q. Did you know then that the boat had been captured?

A. Not until he spoke.

Q. Who was he speaking to?

A. He was speaking to the passengers.

Q. Were you a passenger on board?

A. Yes, sir.

Q. Did you notice what kind of a cord or string he had round his hat?

A. I could not state.

Q. Was there any tassel on it?

A. I could not say.

Q. Was there any gold in it?

A. I don't know.

Q. Did you notice what kind of buttons he had on his coat or vest?

A. No, sir, I don't recollect.

Q. Did the man who said he was a rebel prisoner, say that he was an officer in the Confederate army?

A. I don't recollect.

Q. Where were you put ashore?

A. On Middle Bass Island.

Q. Did these persons in possession show any flag at any time while they were aboard?

A. I did not see any.

Q. Have you ever seen a secession flag?

A. No, sir.

Q. What kind of a box was this of yours that they threw overboard?

A. A large box containing bedding.

Q. Who threw it overboard?

A. I could not state who threw it overboard, but I saw the man pitch it out.

Q. Did either of them say any thing at the time as to why they threw it out?

A. No sir, they were out six or seven rods from the shore.

The accused said he had no further questions to ask the witness.

No questions were asked by the Commission.

The testimony being read to him he affirmed the same.

The Judge Advocate then called DAVID H. THOMAS, a witness for the prosecution, who, being duly sworn, testifies as follows:

Q. State your name, residence, and occupation.

A. My name is David H. Thomas; I reside at Niagara City, Niagara County, New York; occupation, a police officer, by authority of said village.

Q. You arrested the accused?

A. I did, sir.

Q. When and where?

A. In the depot of the New York Central Railroad Company at Niagara City, on the 16th day of December last, at about 9 or 10 o'clock at night.

Q. Did you arrest any other person at the same time?

A. I did, sir, a young man calling himself Anderson.

Q. Were the two in company?

Q. They were. There was another police officer with me at the time of the arrest, Mr. Saule.

Q. What baggage if any, had these men?

A. They had a small carpet bag—contents, a dirty shirt, a shirt that had been worn, a pair of socks, some five or six tallow-candles that had not been burned, some matches done up in a paper, and a box partly full of paper collars. The accused had a bottle of laudanum in one of his pockets.

Q. What was the dress of the accused?

A. I should judge the same clothes that he has on now, with the addition of an overcoat and cap.

Q. He had on citizen's dress?

A. Yes, sir, all citizen's dress, with an overcoat and cap.

Q. Had he any arms about him?

A. He had one of Colt's navy revolvers in a sheath attached to his body by a belt under both his coats, outside of his pants on his hips.

Q. Was the revolver loaded?

A. Yes, sir, it was fully loaded—it was a six-shooter.

Q. Did you inquire his name.

A. I did, sir—while searching him I asked him his name, and he said Beall. A few minutes afterwards I asked him again, with a view of learning his initials; he then said his name was W. W. Baker. I attempted to correct him by stating that he formerly told me his name was Beall, and he denied it. I insisted upon it that he did say Beall, and I told him I should make the record Beall or Baker—I should put his name down Beall or Baker.

Q. If he had money, state what it was?

A. He had two ten-dollar American gold pieces, two four-dollar Canada notes, one two-dollar Canada note, and he had some five or six dollars in American money or scrip, the exact amount I disremember. By scrip I mean fractional currency. I think he had some little silver with him. I did not get the correct amount of the money.

Q. Did he give you any account of himself at any time? and if so, what did he say?

A. When I arrested him he asked me what I arrested him for? My reply to him was, that he knew probably as well as I did what I arrested him for. He said he did not. I finally told him I arrested him as an escaped rebel prisoner. He asked from where. I told him that mattered not, as long as he was an escaped rebel prisoner. Finally he wanted to know from where. He asked if it was from Point Lookout. I told him it was; that he was an escaped prisoner from Point Lookout. Said he, "That I will acknowledge. I am an escaped prisoner from Point Lookout."

Q. Did you make any inquiry of him how he got that Canada money?

A. I did, sir. His answer was, that after he escaped from Point

Lookout he made his way to Baltimore, and he had friends in Baltimore who had furnished him with this money to go to Canada.

Q. In regard to the carpet-bag of which you have spoken, and the contents, what are the facts within your knowledge as stated by either of the two parties you arrested, that will enable the Court to judge to whom it belonged?

A. When we arrested the two men, this bag was between them on the seat, and carried, I think, by the prisoner Anderson into the room where we took them to search them. It was into the adjoining room, the telegraph office, that we took them to search them. We asked which of them owned that bag, and the young man said that the accused owned the bag.

Q. The accused being present and hearing the remark?

A. Yes, sir; I asked him if the bag was his, and he said it was not. The accused said it was not; but the other man said it was.

Q. Did you make any inquiry as to the purpose of the candles or matches?

A. I asked them what they were doing with those candles. They said they were sometimes a necessary article to use when they could not get other lights. This young man, Anderson I think, answered in that way. I would not want to say which of them; it was between them. They were both present. In regard to the laudanum, I asked the accused what he was doing with that; and his answer was, that he was subject to the toothache.

Q. If the accused said any thing to you in regard to the mode of his arrest in connection with the fact of his being armed, state what he said.

A. Yes, sir. During the evening or night, when we were conversing over the subject, he said it was fortunate that I arrested him suddenly as I did; that he had been in prison so much that he had made up his mind, whenever he was attempted to be arrested again; and on this particular occasion, had I not taken him as quick as I did, that one or the other of us would have been a dead man—that he had fully resolved never to be taken alive.

Cross-examined by the Accused.

Q. Was Beall alone when you arrested him?

A. No, sir; they were together sitting on a settee, he and Anderson, in the depot of the Central Railroad at that place.

Q. Was it day or night?

A. Night, somewhere between 9 and 10 o'clock—about 10 o'clock.

Q. Was any person with you?

A. Mr. Saule, another policeman.

Q. Did he take any part in making the arrest?
A. He put his hand on Anderson, and I mine on Beall.
Q. How large was this vial of laudanum that he had?
A. I believe what they call a two-ounce vial.
Q. Was it full?
A. There was a very little out of it.
Q. In this conversation that he had with you did he tell you any thing about his being a Confederate officer?
A. He said that he belonged to the Second Virginia Infantry, was a sergeant in the ranks. I asked him if he held any other position, and he said, No.
Q. Did he tell you when he escaped from Point Lookout?
A. He did not give me the dates, but it was several days previous to his arrival at Buffalo.
Q. What kind of a cap was he in?
A. It was a cloth cap—a citizen's cap.

The accused said he had no further questions to ask the witness.

No questions by the Commission. His testimony being read to the witness, he affirmed the same.

The Commission then adjourned until to-morrow at 11 o'clock, A.M.

JOHN A. BOLLES, Major and A.D.C.,
Judge Advocate.

Fort Lafayette, New York Harbor,
Thursday, *February 2d,* 1864.

The Commission met pursuant to adjournment.

Present all the members.

Present, also, the Judge Advocate, and the accused, John Y. Beall, who was brought in for trial; and James T. Brady, Esq., his counsel.

Yesterday's proceedings were read and approved.

The Judge Advocate then called EDWARD HAYS, a witness for the prosecution, who being duly sworn, in presence of the accused, testified as follows:

Q. State your name and occupation.
A. Edward Hays, doorman at the Police Headquarters, Mulberry Street.
Q. You see the accused sitting here; have you ever seen him before? and if so, where?
A. Yes, sir; at the Police Headquarters in Mulberry Street.
Q. State whether he ever said any thing to you, and if so, what, in regard to his escape from Mulberry Street?

A. He asked me to carry a letter out for him and have it mailed, I asked him where he wanted to send the letter to; he said he wanted it to go to Canada; I asked him if he could get it through easily there; he said he did not think he could very easily, as the Government were opening all letters which were going there now; he said he thought if he could get a letter to Canada, and word could be sent to his Government that he was in prison, they might do some good for him to get him out. I then went to get him the paper to write the letter; at the same time I reported to Mr. Kelso, who was then in charge of the Detective Office, what he had told me, and I went back to the prisoner and told him that there were several detectives in the office at the time, that I could not very easily get the paper; that I would wait for a start to get the office cleared of those detectives, and then I would have a better opportunity of getting it in without being seen. He then said to me: "Hays, I tell you what you can do for me;" I said, "What?" he said, "You can let me go;" I said I could not; he said, "If you do I will give you $1,000 in gold." I asked him if he had that amount of money with him; he said no, but if I would take his word, his word was good for the money when he would get to Canada; that a man there had that amount of money and more belonging to him; that it would surely be given as soon as he would get there. I asked him if he had any hand in the fires here in New York; he said no, but that he knew the parties, and that they were then in Canada. I told him I did not think I could let him go for the money, as it would place me in a bad position; that I did not like to do it; that it would be too much risk for me to run. He said that I knew his position; how he was placed; that he thought he would be found guilty, and that I should run a little risk to save him. He said he was arrested before, some time ago, and that he got a letter through by some of his friends, and the Confederate Government hearing of his imprisonment here, put in prison a son of one of General Meade's head officers, together with eleven more officers, and kept them there until he was released. I then said to him, "I suppose if your Government found out that you were in prison here now that they would try to get you out in some way." He said he did not think they would, because he was arrested under a different charge now from what he was then, and that he did not think his Government was as strong now as it was then. I then told him I would see if I could let him go; that I could not say whether I' could or not; I asked him if he did not want to write a letter out, and he said no, that it would take too long before the letter could do any good, but that I could release him without getting myself into any trouble; and said he, "You know you can." I then left him and came into the office; I told him that I would see what I could do, and I reported to

Mr. Kelso and Inspector Carpenter what he had told me. I again went back to him and told him that I thought it was pretty hard for me to do it, but if I did it what time in the night would he like to get away. He said he would like to get away in the fore part of the night; that he had two friends living up, he thought, in Thirtieth Street; that if he could get to their house, he wanted to get out in time so he could get there, so nobody would hear him make a noise around the place; he thought he could get arms there, and then it would take somebody to arrest him if he could get arms after he got out; for, said he, "I know well what would happen to me if I was to be caught and brought back again." I then asked him if those friends of his could not furnish him the money before he would leave New York. He said that very probably they could furnish a part of it, probably half of it in greenbacks, if not in gold, before he would leave New York; if not, that he would leave me an order that would positively get it in Canada. I asked him how did he think he could get clear from New York, and if he had any friends that he thought would get him clear on the way going. He said first he would go to this man's house in Thirtieth Street, and then he would start for a friend of his in Jersey, about five miles from Jersey City, who did business in New York, who came every morning and went back at night, and by getting there he knew he would be safe. I then asked him if he would not tell me the number of the house where those men lived in Thirtieth Street, or what were their names, who were willing to assist him. He would not tell me their names; said he did not know exactly the street they lived in, or the number of the house. I asked him what his own name was, or if he gave the right name in the detective's office when they brought him in. He said he did not; that they did not know his name, and could not find it out. I then said to him: "I think you are a very smart man, and you must have done a good deal of harm to our Government since this war commenced;" and he said: "Yes, I have taken hundreds and hundreds of prisoners; I have done Lincoln's Government a good deal of harm, and they know it." I asked him if it was on land or sea that he took those prisoners, and he said that it was his secret. I asked him to tell me his right name, and he said he would not. He said he knew something that would be worth $30,000 to any one in the detective's office, if he would tell, and things that would be worth millions of dollars to the Government if he would only come out and discover, but he said he would die first; he said he knew he could not live long, as he had got a ball through his side, and he knew that would come against him and cause death anyhow. I told him, "I am very glad you are not very fond of telling or discovering, for you would have to keep a good record if I let you go." He said he knew many things that he would not tell; he said,

"You can rest assured that you can get the $1,000, and get it in gold, as I own more than that myself." I then told him I would see what I could do, and if I could let him out that night I would, if possible, but I could not exactly say; and that if not, I would come back and see him the following evening; and I then left him, and when I came back he was gone, and I have not seen him since; he was taken to Fort Lafayette the next day.

No further questions by Judge Advocate.

The accused objected to the testimony of the witness in which he narrated the statement of the accused, as irrelevant, not relating to any charge or specification, but did not wish any ruling on the point.

Cross-examined by Accused.

Q. How long have you been doorkeeper at the Police Headquarters?

A. Since the 11th of April last.

Q. What was your business before that?

A. I worked in the Navy Yard at laboring work.

Q. Where did you reside when you were appointed doorkeeper?

A. At 17 Lewis Street, New York.

Q. What was your business, if any, before you worked in the Navy Yard?

A. Liquor business, at 157 Madison Street.

Q. About what was the date at which you first saw Beall, the accused?

A. It must have been a week before New Year's, I think. I think it was New Year's Day that I was to come here and see him. It was the night before New Year's that this conversation occurred. I am not positive, but I think so.

Q. Did all the conversation you have stated occur on the night before New Year's?

A. It all passed in one night.

Q. In what part of the headquarters was Beall confined at that time?

A. Down stairs in the cell.

Q. Who had charge of the cell?

A. Mr. Kelso was then in charge of the office, in the absence of Mr. Young.

Q. Who had the key of the cell?

A. The keys were generally left in the office. When I would be on duty as door-man, I would take the keys when I wanted to go into the cell for any thing, to feed them, etc. I am doorkeeper one day, and another man the next day.

Q. How did you happen to begin this conversation with Beall?

A. Mr. Kelso asked me if I could not find out what Beall's name was; and if I could get him to tell his name, to try and find out what charges he was arrested on, and what was against him.

Q. Where were the Police Commissioners at that time?

A. I don't know, sir, if they were not gone home from Headquarters. I don't know if they were up-stairs or not.

Q. At what hour of the night was it that Kelso asked you to find out Beall's name?

A. I think it must have been about 7 o'clock.

Q. Did Kelso say that he did not know what Beall was charged with?

A. No, sir, he did not say any such thing.

Q. Did he say that he did not know what his name was.

A. He did not say so.

Q. Did he speak of him as a person named Beall?

A. No, sir, not at that time.

Q. I want you to repeat what Kelso said to you, when he expressed a wish that you should see this man and ascertain his name?

A. Mr. Kelso said to me when I would get time to go into the cell to him, to see if I could not draw on with him to get him to tell me what his name was; and if so, to see if I could not get from him to tell me what charges he was arrested on. That was all Mr. Kelso said to me.

Q. How did Kelso describe or make you understand what person you were to ask this question of?

A. Baker; he told me to go in and see Baker—which name he then went under; I called him Baker always when he was there; he went by the name of Baker; he told me to go in and see Baker and see what I could learn from him.

Q. Before Kelso spoke to you did you know that there was any such person as Baker confined in any cell there?

A. I knew that he was there and that he went by the name of Baker—that he was called Baker.

Q. Who told you that he was called Baker?

A. I heard it from the detectives first when they first brought him in there.

Q. Had you seen him before the time when Kelso asked you to go and inquire about his name?

A. Yes, sir; several times.

Q. Did Kelso tell you what object he had in finding out this man's name?

A. No, sir.

Q. What was Kelso's position there at that time?

A. He was then acting as sergeant.

Q. Did you say to him that if he wanted to know what this man's name was, or what he was charged with, he could ask the Commissioners?

A. No, sir.

Q. Did you know who brought Baker in?

A. Not at that time.

Q. Did Kelso state that he had asked the Commissioners what Baker was charged with, and that they would not tell him?

A. No, sir.

Q. Then he gave no reason whatever for wishing to obtain this information?

A. No, sir; not that I know of.

Q. Did you, at Mr. Kelso's request, go immediately to the cell where the accused was?

A. Not immediately—I waited some time until I had leisure; I had a good deal of work to do.

Q. Was it a part of your general instructions that you should or should not converse with prisoners there?

A. I never got any instructions to that effect as to whether to converse with them or not.

Q. What time of night was it that you went to the accused and began this conversation with him?

A. I should think it must be about eight o'clock—I think so, I'm not sure—between seven and nine.

Q. Was that the first time you had ever spoken a word with him?

A. I had spoken to him previously to that while feeding him, and every thing of that kind.

Q. Had you done any thing before that to get his confidence, or had he done any thing to get yours?

A. No, sir; not that I know of.

Q. Had you in any way before that night said or intimated to him that you were willing to help him to escape?

A. No, sir.

Q. Can you state any reason growing out of what had passed between you and the accused why he should place any confidence in you particularly?

A. I did not know of any reason why he should have done it.

Q. When you went at 8 o'clock to his cell to obtain for Mr. Kelso the information Kelso said he wanted, what was the first remark that you made to the accused that you now remember?

A. There was a man in the cell that day, an old man, who wanted me to take a letter for him, and I would not take it; he said he would pay for taking it; I asked how much he would pay, and he said "so much"—I forget how much he did say; I said I could not send it for that; that evening when I went in at 8 o'clock in the cell, there was no one there at that time but the accused; I said to this man, the accused: "It is pretty cold in here this evening;" he said "Yes, it was pretty cold;" I said, "The old man had good luck to get out of there before night, as it was so cold;" he said "Yes;" I said he wanted me to send a letter for him, and I could not do it; he would not give enough to have it sent, and I could not get anybody to take it for that amount; the accused said, "I wish you would take a letter for me and I will pay well for taking it;" I told him, "There is a good deal done for money—money does a good deal;" I then asked him where he wanted to have the letter sent; that was how it commenced.

Q. Had you any instructions whether to permit any letter to be sent by a prisoner without its being examined by any of the public officers of the Government or City.

A. Yes, sir; I was instructed not to take a letter out for him without first showing it to the officer in charge of the detectives' desk.

Q. Did you know that the accused when first taken to the headquarters of the police had been searched, and that he had no money about him or under his command at the time this conversation took place?

A. I don't know; they did not tell me they searched him; I know it is customary to search prisoners when they come here.

Q. Up to the time when you returned the first time to his cell that night and said that you could not get the paper for him to write on, had you said any thing to him about his name?

A. I don't think I had.

Q. Up to that time had you asked him what he was charged with?

A. I don't think I had.

Q. Did you during any part of this conversation ask him what he was charged with?

A. Yes, sir.

Q. What did he say?

A. He said that was his secret.

Q. Do you mean to say that he stated that what he was charged with by our Government was his secret?

A. What he was charged with—the charge he was arrested on? Yes, sir.

Q. Did he state that as the reason why he could not tell you what he was charged with?

A. He did not state what was the reason; he would not tell me.

Q. Did you tell Kelso that he had refused to tell you what he was charged with?

A. Yes, sir; I think so.

Q. Did you bring him paper to write on?

A. No, sir.

Q. Did he write, or attempt to write any letter?

A. No, sir; not that night.

Q. Did you pretend to him that if he wrote a letter you would have it sent for him to Canada?

A. I told him I would have it taken, and try and send it to Canada.

Q. Did you intend to send it to Canada when you said so?

A. I first intended to give it to Kelso, who was in charge, to let him act on it as he saw fit.

Q. Did Kelso during that night give you any instructions about the subjects about which you should talk to the accused?

A. After I first came in and reported, he told me to try to find out the charges he was arrested on, and to get from him all I could.

Q. Did you report to Kelso, from time to time that night, what the accused said?

A. Yes, sir; I reported.

Q. Did Kelso suggest to you to get the accused to tell you he wanted to escape?

A. He told me no such thing.

Q. Before the accused said to you, "You can let me go," what, if any thing, had you said or done to make him believe that you were his friend and would let him go?

A. Nothing that I could think of, more than I would see and have that letter forwarded as much as possible.

Q. Do you mean to say that although he refused to tell what his name was, he wanted you to take his word for $1,000 in gold to let him escape?

A. He wanted me to take his word. Yes, sir; he was to leave me an order for the money on that man in Canada.

Q. Did you ask him whether he would sign his real name to that order?

A. No, I don't think I did.

Q. Did you say to him that he could not expect you to take his word when he would not give his name?

A. I don't think I said so.

Q. When you asked him about the fires in New York did you do that of your own suggestion, or because Kelso mentioned it?

A. No; I thought I would find out if possible who the parties were, as I would like to know it at that time.

Q. When he told you that he thought he would be found guilty, did he say what he would be found guilty of?

A. No, sir.

Q. When he told you that he had been arrested before, did he tell you where he was arrested or what he was arrested for?

A. He did not say.

Q. Did he tell you the name of one of General Meade's head officers whose son had been imprisoned by his Government?

A. He told me the name and I have forgotten it.

Q. When he spoke of his two friends who resided in 30th Street, did he say in what part of the street they lived, or what their business was, or any thing of that kind?

A. He said he did not know in what part of the street they lived in, or if they lived in 30th Street or not; he said they did business down town in the lower part of the city.

No further questions by the accused.

No question was asked by the Commission. His testimony being read to the witness, he affirmed the same.

The Judge Advocate then called GEORGE S. ANDERSON, who being duly sworn, in presence of the accused, testified as follows:

Q. What are your name and age?

A. George S. Anderson; I will be eighteen some day this month.

Q. Have you been in the Confederate military service?

A. Yes, sir.

Q. You saw and spoke to the accused as you came in; when did you see him the last time before?

A. I saw him yesterday, and the last time I saw him before that was in prison in New York City.

Q. When and where did you first see Captain Beall, the accused?

A. I first saw him on the railroad out from Buffalo, several miles west towards Dunkirk; I don't know what day it was; it was five or six days before my arrest at Suspension Bridge.

Q. Were you and the accused arrested at Suspension Bridge at the same time?

A. Yes, sir.

Q. State the circumstances which led to your seeing the accused on the railroad, and all that followed after you saw him in connection with your movements and his.

The accused inquired if this testimony would relate to the sixth specification of the first charge. The Judge Advocate answered that it would.

The accused objected to any proof in regard to that specification, on the ground that it related to a transaction which, if perpetrated as stated in the specification, would be an offence cognizable by the laws of the State of New York, and not within the jurisdiction of any military tribunal; he consented that the objection be overruled for the present, but he wished to reserve the point. The question being repeated, the witness answered as follows:

A. I got to Buffalo on the Sunday preceding my arrest; I got there an hour or two before daylight on Sunday morning; I went into a hotel and got a room and went to bed; I was in citizen's dress and had no arms; in the morning, I suppose it was 8 o'clock when I got up, I went into the street and then came back to the hotel.

Q. Did you meet any one at the hotel whom you had known in the rebel service? and if so, whom?

A. I did; I met Lieutenant Headley; he belonged to Morgan's command when I knew him; I saw him, but I did not speak to him, and he did not speak to me; he got up and went out on the street, and I went out after him after a while; he signified to me to follow him out; I went out after him and he told me to follow him up stairs in the same hotel, which I did; I also saw Colonel Martin there who had been an officer in the rebel service.

Q. What passed between you and them?

A. They said they were glad to see me; they said they had a plan in view then, and they wanted more men, and they would like to have me with them.

Q. What did they say about their plan, if any thing?

A. They said they intended to capture a train; they told me to remain there that day; that they were going to Dunkirk the next day to capture the train from Dunkirk the next night after that.

Q. Where did you get the pistol that was found upon you when you were arrested?

A. Lieutenant Headley gave it to me.

Q. On this Sunday or afterwards?

A. No, sir; it was afterwards at Dunkirk.

Q. Did they tell you where they had come from?

A. No, sir; they did not.

Q. Whether from Canada or any other place?

A. I think they said they were from Canada.

Q. What, if any thing, did they say to you in regard to their intended movements, after they had accomplished their plan?

A. They did not say any thing; they expected to go back to Canada, but what they intended to do they did not say any thing about.

Q. Go on with your narrative of what was done.

A. On Tuesday evening I went to Dunkirk, and they were to capture the train that night coming from Dunkirk to Buffalo.

Q. Who went to Dunkirk?

A. I went to Dunkirk, and these two officers went.

Q. Anybody else that you know of?

A. Not that I know of; at Dunkirk they told me that they were not going to try to take the train that night; they told me to be at the depot in Buffalo the next day at 2 o'clock; that was Wednesday. I was there at the depot the next day at 2 o'clock, and I saw those two officers there, and they told me to follow them out along the railroad towards Dunkirk, which I did; I followed them out I suppose three or four miles from the town, when we overtook Captain Beall, the accused, on the railroad.

Q. State whether Beall became one of the party from that time in their movements.

A. Yes, sir, he was one of the party. We went on the railroad to a point I suppose five or six miles from the city—we four; we tried to get a rail off the track.

Q. How did you try?

A. We tried with a large sledge-hammer and a cold chisel.

Q. In whose possession did you first see that sledge-hammer?

A. I saw it in Capt. Beall's possession.

Q. Who used it in trying to lift the rail from the track?

A. Colonel Martin.

Q. Who else?

A. I don't think that anybody else used it. We tried to get a rail off the track and could not do it—did not succeed in the attempt, and went back to town. We then went to Canada that night, to Port Colburn. We remained there two nights and one day. We then came back to Buffalo. There was five in the party then.

Q. The same four with one additional man?

A. Yes, sir.

Q. Who was he?

A. I don't know who he was.

Q. Do you know what he was from his own statement or otherwise; whether he was a soldier or officer in the rebel service?

A. He was a soldier.

Q. How do you know?

A. All I know about it was, he told me he was an escaped prisoner from Rock Island.

Q. You five came to Buffalo, and what was then done?

A. The Colonel told me to go with this Capt. Beall and stay with him, and he would meet us at a bridge with a sleigh—which I did.

Q. Did Col. Martin meet you there?

A. Yes, sir, and Lieut. Headley was with him.

Q. Where was the fifth man?

A. The fifth man went with Capt. Beall and me, and we parted. We missed the bridge—went the other side of the bridge, and we took one end of the road and came back to the bridge, and he took the other end of the road, and the sleigh had got by when we arrived there. But the sleigh found us at last.

Q. And then there were five of you?

A. Yes, sir, five of us—the same five as before.

Q. What did you do then?

A. We went to a point on the railroad I suppose five miles from the city.

Q. And did what?

A. We did not do any thing; the train passed about the time that we got there.

Q. What did you do that night and the next day?

A. We went back to Buffalo, and I and Capt. Beall and this fifth man stayed together at the hotel until the next day at 2 o'clock.

Q. What did you do then?

A. Then we met the Colonel and Lieut. Headley in a sleigh at the same bridge, the next day at 2 o'clock.

Q. The same party of five, and the same sleigh?

A. Yes, sir; it was a two-horse sleigh. Then we went back to the same point on the railroad that we went to on the day before.

Q. What did you do there?

A. Three of the party went up the track to get the sledge-hammer, I think, and I and the Colonel were in the sleigh. We hitched the horses and got out, and went up the railroad a piece, and we saw the train coming, and the Colonel had taken up an iron rail and taken one end and laid it across the track. He got the rail by the side of the track.

Q. How far had he got it on the track?

A. He laid it across the track.

Q. Was it then light or dark?

A. It was then just about dark.

Q. What happened, so far as you saw, to the train?

A. I saw it strike the rail; and the whistle blew just then, and it stopped, I suppose, some two or three hundred yards from there. I don't know what damage was done.

Q. What did your party do, or what did the people in the cars do?

A. Somebody came back with a lantern—two or three came back. We went back to the sleigh and went to Buffalo.

Q. What became of the sledge-hammer?

A. It was thrown away; I don't think they got it.

Q. What became of the cold chisel?

A. It was thrown away.

Q. What had the cold chisel been carried in?

A. It had been carried in the carpet-bag.

Q. In the carpet-bag that was taken when you and the accused were arrested?

A. Yes, sir.

Q. In whose possession did you first see that carpet-bag?

A. I saw in Lieut. Headley's possession.

Q. How came it to be in your possession or Capt. Beall's at the time of your arrest?

A. It belonged to the party, I suppose.

Q. Who brought it away from the place of the railroad collision with the rail?

A. It was in the sleigh.

Q. On getting back to Buffalo with the sleigh, what became of the party?

A. They determined to leave and go to Canada; we took the cars for Suspension Bridge.

Q. Who brought along the carpet-bag?

A. I think I had it most of the time.

Q. By whose direction?

A. By the direction of the party.

Q. On getting to Suspension Bridge on the train from Buffalo, what was done?

A. I and Captain Beall were arrested.

Q. What became of the other three?

A. I don't know; I never saw them after I left Buffalo.

Q. You and Captain Beall stopped at the depot, and were arrested there?

A. Yes, sir.

Q. Did you hear the statement that Captain Beall made to the police officers who arrested you and him as to where he came from, and who he was? State as near as you can recollect all that was said and done at the time of your arrest.

A. Captain Beall told the officer that we were from Point Lookout; he said that we had escaped from Point Lookout, and were making our way to Canada. I have most forgotten what was said there at the time.

Q. What time in the evening was it that you were arrested?

A. We were arrested about 9 or 10 o'clock at night; I and Captain Beall were in the depot seated near together.

Q. How many officers were there who made the arrest?

A. There were but two officers, I think.

Q. Were you and Captain Beall wide awake when they came in and made the arrest?

A. I was asleep; I don't know how he was.

Q. What awoke you?

A. The officers awoke me; they pulled me off my seat.

Q. Where was the carpet-bag at that time?

A. It was on the bench that I was sitting on.

Q. Between you and Captain Beall?

A. Yes, sir; I think it was.

Q. When Captain Beall stated that you were from Point Lookout, did you say any thing? and if so, what?

A. I think that I assented to what he said, but I did not give any account of myself.

Q. Did Colonel Martin, or Lieutenant Headley, or the accused, at any time in your presence state whether they were under orders, or were acting by anybody's directions?

A. No, sir; I don't think they did.

Q. What, if any thing, did they tell you they intended or expected to do or accomplish at any or all times when you were with them in or near Buffalo?

A. They did not tell me any thing except about the train.

Q. What did they say about that?

A. The colonel told me that he expected to capture the express and the money that was on it.

Q. Is that all you recollect?

A. That is all I recollect.

No further questions by the Judge Advocate.

Cross-examination by Accused.

Q. In what part of Virginia were you born?

A. I was born in Pittsylvania County.

Q. How long have you known Captain Beall?

A. The first time I ever saw him was on the railroad.

Q. When did you first enter the service of the Confederate States?

A. I entered it last May, I think.

Q. What corps were you in, and in whose command?

A. In Morgan's; as a private in the cavalry.

Q. When did you become acquainted with Col. Martin?
A. I got acquainted with him when I was with the command.
Q. Was he a colonel in Morgan's corps?
A. He was with Morgan.
Q. Did you attach yourself to Martin as courier or otherwise?
A. Yes, sir; I was courier for the Colonel.
Q. How long did you remain his courier?
A. I think it was a week or two.
Q. Then what became of you?
A. I went back to my company.
Q. At what place?
A. It was about three miles above Rogersville in Tennessee, I think, where I joined my company.
Q. Had you ever seen Lieut. Headley before you joined him at Buffalo?
A. Yes, sir; he was with Colonel Martin.
Q. You had seen him and knew him personally?
A. Yes, sir; he was attached to my company about three weeks.
Q. When you went into the hotel with Col. Martin, and it was said that there was a plan in view—who said that there was a plan in view?
A. It was the Colonel; I think both of them were speaking of it at the time, and spoke to me.
Q. Did the Colonel introduce you to Headley?
A. No; I was acquainted with Headley before.
Q. Was any thing said about there being three or some other number of Confederate generals on the express train of the Lake Shore Road, and who were being removed from Johnson's Island to Fort Warren, Massachusetts?
A. No, sir; there was not.
Q. Colonel Martin had command of this expedition?
A. Yes, sir.
Q. And Headley and Capt. Beall acted under his orders?
A. Yes, sir; all that I saw acted under his orders.
Q. Was Capt. Beall present at the time when it was said what this plan was they had in view about the capture of the train?
A. No, sir; he was not.
Q. Was the accused present at any conversation between Headley and Martin, when you were also present?
A. I don't think that he was; I don't think that we had any conversation in his presence.
Q. Had you ever seen Capt. Beall before the time that you overtook him on the railroad?

A. I never had; not that I know of.

Q. Who told you what his name was?

A. They told me that he was one of the party, and they gave me some name.

Q. Who told you?

A. Lieutenant Headley told me.

Q. Did they tell you that he was an officer in the Confederate service, or about his rank, or any thing of that kind?

A. I don't think they did.

Q. Did they call him Captain, or how did they address him?

A. I have forgotten how they did address him.

Q. Did Captain Beall give you any orders in regard to the attempt to get the rail off the track?

A. No, sir; I don't think he did.

Q. Who gave those orders?

A. Colonel Martin was the principal; I think he gave the orders; it all went by his directions.

Q. When the train struck the rail which Colonel Martin had laid across the track, was your party concealed somewhere?

A. Yes, sir, we were in the woods; I and the Colonel were in the woods; the others, I think, were up the road apiece; I don't know whether they were concealed or not.

Q. Did you all come together again after the train struck?

A. Yes, sir.

Q. Was that at the place where the sleigh had been left?

A. Yes, sir.

Q. And went back to Buffalo?

A. Yes, sir.

Q. Arriving there about what time?

A. Well, sir, we got there, I suppose, an hour after dark; it was about dark when this thing happened, and we went on to Buffalo.

Q. Did you go into the hotel together, or did you separate outside after you got back to Buffalo?

A. I don't recollect whether we went into any hotels or not.

Q. You say the party determined to go to Canada?

A. Yes, sir.

Q. What arrangement was made, if any, about your meeting in Canada, you five people?

A. There was not any arrangement made about meeting; they were all to go, I think, to Toronto.

Q. Why did you not all go together?

A. There was nothing said, that I recollect, about the reason why we did not go together.

Q. In going from Buffalo to Niagara you were all on the same train?

A. I suppose we were, but I don't recollect seeing them after we left Buffalo.

Q. When you and Beall were in the depot at Niagara, what were you waiting for?

A. We were waiting for the train—the eleven o'clock train that night; I think it was the eleven o'clock train.

Q. Was that the only reason why you were in the depot at that time—waiting for the train?

A. Yes, sir, that is all the reason that I know of.

The accused proposed no further questions.

Examination by the Commission.

Q. What do you mean by Express?

A. The Express and the money in it.

Q. What do you understand to be the meaning; that they were to take the Express train, or the Express in the train?

A. The Express that I understood was the Express safe.

Q. What did the accused do at the time Col. Martin laid the rail across the track?

A. He did nothing; there was nobody that did any thing except Colonel Martin.

The Court proposed no further questions; his testimony being read to the witness, he affirmed the same.

The Judge Advocate then read in evidence the three letters of the accused, and acknowledged by him to be his, which were placed by him in the hands of Col. Burke: one addressed to Colonel Jacob Thompson, Toronto, Canada West, dated January 22, 1865; one addressed, by Flag of Truce, to Messrs. Hunter & Lucas, 173 Main Street, Richmond, Virginia, same date; and the third addressed to Colonel A. R. Boteler, Richmond, Virginia, by a Flag of Truce, same date; which three letters are hereto annexed, and marked Exhibits A, B, and C.

The Judge Advocate also read in evidence a pocket diary, which the accused said was kept by him, and was in his own handwriting, and taken from him at Fort Lafayette, commencing Thursday, Dec. 29, 1864. It is hereto annexed and marked Exhibit D. The Judge Advocate announced that the prosecution rested here.

The accused being asked if he was ready to proceed with his defence, answered that he was not, and asked for an adjournment until next week.

On motion of a member of the Commission the further hearing of the case was postponed until Tuesday, February 7, 1865, at 11 o'clock, A.M.

The Commission then adjourned until to-morrow at 11 o'clock, A.M., to meet at Headquarters, New York City.

JOHN A. BOLLES, Major and A.D.C.,
Judge Advocate.

Fort Lafayette, N. Y. Harbor,
Feb. 7, 1865, 11 o'clock, A.M.

The Commission met according to adjournment.

Present, all the members, the Judge Advocate, the accused, J. Y. Beall, and his counsel.

The proceedings of the two last days of this trial were read and approved.

The accused then introduced the papers hereto annexed, marked Exhibits E and F, purporting to be copies of the warrant of the appointment of the accused as Master in the insurgent navy, and of a manifesto of the President of the so-called Confederate States; and there the defence rested.

By leave of the Commission, the counsel for the accused, James T. Brady, Esq., then delivered in behalf of the accused the address hereto annexed, and marked Exhibit G.

Upon the conclusion of the address of the accused by his counsel, the Judge Advocate, in behalf of the prosecution, delivered the address hereto annexed, and marked Exhibit H.

The Commission then adjourned to meet to-morrow, Feb. 8, 1865, at the Department Headquarters, New York City, at 12 o'clock noon.

JOHN A. BOLLES, Major and A.D.C.,
Judge Advocate.

Department Headquarters, New York City,
Feb. 8, 1865, 12 o'clock noon.

The Commission met pursuent to adjournment. Present all the members, and the Judge Advocate.

The Commission was cleared for deliberation upon the case of the accused, John Y. Beall.

Upon careful consideration of the evidence adduced, the Commission find the accused, John Y. Beall, as follows:

Of Specification 1, Charge I., . . . Guilty.
" " 2, " . . . Guilty.
" " 3, " . . . Guilty.
" " 4, " . . . Guilty.
" " 5, " . . . Guilty.
" " 6, " . . . Guilty.
Of CHARGE I, ... Guilty.

Of Specification 1, Charge II., . . . Guilty.
" " 2, " . . . Guilty.
" " 3, " . . . Not Guilty.
on the day alleged in this specification:
Of CHARGE II., ... Guilty.

And the Commission do therefore sentence him, the said John Y. Beall, to be hanged by the neck until dead, at such time and place as the General in Command of the Department may direct, two-thirds of the members concurring therein.

FITZ HENRY WARREN, Brig.-Gen. U. S. Vols.,
President.
JOHN A. BOLLES, Major and A.D.C.,
Judge-Advocate.

Exhibit A.

One U. S. Stamp enclosed.]

Fort Lafayette, N. Y., *Jan.* 22*d*, 1865.

Mr. D. B. LUCAS,
173 Main St., Richmond, Va.

DEAR DAN:—I have taken up board and lodging at this famous establishment. I was captured in Decr. last, and spent Xmas in the Metropolitan Hd. Qrs. Police Station. I am now being tried for irregular warfare, by a Military Commission, a species of court.

The acts are said to have been committed on Lake Erie and the Canada frontier. You know that I am not a "guerrillero" or "spy." I desire you to get the necessary evidence that I am in the Confederate service, regularly, and forward it to me at once. I shall write to Cols. Boteler and Holliday in regard to this matter. I must have this evidence. As the Commission so far have acted fairly, I am confident of an acquittal. Has Will been exchanged? I saw that Steadman had been killed in Kentucky. Alas! how they fall! Please let my family know if possible of my whereabouts. Where is my Georgia friend? Have you heard any thing from her since I left? May God bless her. I should like so much to hear from her, from home, Will, and yourself. Be so kind, therefore, as to attend at once to this business for me. Remember me to any and all of my friends that you may see.

Send me some postage stamps for my correspondence.

Hoping soon to hear from you,
I remain your friend,
J. Y. BEALL, *C. S. N.*

If Mr. Lucas is not in Richmond, will Mr. HUNTER ATTEND to this AT ONCE.

Exhibit B.

[I enclose a U. S. Stamp.]

Fort Lafayette, N. Y., *Jan. 22d*, 1865.

Col. A. R. Boteler,
  Richmond, Va.

Dear Sir:—I am on trial before a Military Commission for irregular warfare, as a "guerrillero" and "spy." The acts are said to have been committed on Lake Erie and at Suspension Bridge, in Sept. and Dec. last.

As I cannot in person procure any papers from Richd., I have to rely on my friends, and therefore I request you to procure evidence of my being regularly in service, and forward such evidence at once to me. I have also written to Messrs. Hunter and Lucas. Please call on them in regard to this, and also Mr. Henderson if necessary.

Very truly, your friend,
J. Y. Beall, *C. S. N.*

Exhibit C.

Fort Lafayette, N. Y., *Jan. 22d*, 1865.

Col. Jacob Thompson,
  Toronto, C. W.

Sir:—I was captured in Decr., and am on trial before a Mititary Commission for irregular warfare, as a "guerrillero" and "spy." The acts are said to have been committed on Lake Erie and at Suspension Bridge, N. Y., in September and December last.

I desire to procure from my Government and its authorities evidence of my being regularly in service, and of having been acting under and by authority. Please procure and forward me, as soon as possible, certificates or other evidence confirming this fact.

The Commission so far have evidenced a disposition to treat me fairly and equitably. With the evidence you can send, together with that I have a right to expect from Richd. and elsewhere, I am confident of an acquittal.

Please attend at once to this, acknowledging at any rate the receipt of this letter.

Very respectfully,
J. Y. Beall,

Exhibit D.

Thursday, Dec. 29, 1864. I purpose to keep in this little book a daily account of my imprisonment as far as I can.

First. As to my incarceration:

I was arrested Friday, December 16th, in the N. Y. Central R. R. station house, at the Suspension Bridge (junction with the Gr. Western R. R. of Canada). I was brought to this city Sunday evening (18th), and lodged here. I have been taken out some half a dozen times to be shown men, whose houses have been attempted by fire, or property otherwise attempted. The *modus operandi* is this: The prisoner, unkept, roughly clad, dirty, and bearing marks of confinement, is placed among well-dressed detectives, and the recognizer is shown in. As a matter of course he can tell who is the stranger. My *home* is a cell about 8 feet by 5, on the ground floor. The floor is stone; the walls brick; the door iron, the upper half grated, and opens into a passage running in front of three other cells; this passage is lighted by two large windows doubly grated, and has an iron door; at night it is lighted with gas. The landscape view from my door, through the window, is that of an area of some 30 feet square. By special arrangement I have a mattrass and blanket. There is a supply of water in my room, and a sink. My meals are brought three times a day, about 9, 3 and 7. My library consists of two New Testaments. I am trying to get a Book of Common Prayer. The first week there were brought to this place 10 persons, charged with criminal offences: men, women, and children. At first I took an interest in their cases, but now I do not; they all have been guilty, I believe, and they all wished me a speedy riddance. Nearly every one I have met with seems to regard society as his enemy, and a just prey. They look on an offence simply a skirmish. Profane, lying and thieving, what a people! Nearly all recommend me to take the oath of allegiance and enter the army and desert. But some are opposed to betraying comrades ("going back on 'em"), while others more liberal advocate any means as legitimate to save oneself from severe punishment. The Christmas of '64 I spent in a New York prison! Had I, 4 years ago, stood in New York, and proclaimed myself a citizen of Virginia, I would have been welcomed; now I am immured because I am a Virginian *tempora mutantur, et cum illis mutamus*. As long as I am a citizen of Virginia, I shall cling to her destiny and maintain her laws as expressed by a majority of her citizens speaking through their authorized channel, if her voice be for war or peace. I shall go as she says. But I would not go for a minority carrying on war in opposition to the majority, as the innocent will suffer and not the guilty; but I do not justify oppression in the majority. What misery have I seen during these four years, murder, lust, hate, rapine, devastation, war! What hardships suffered, what privations endured! May God grant that I may not see the like again! Nay, that my country may not! Oh, far rather would I welcome Death, *come as he might;* far rather would I meet him than go through four more such years. I can now understand why David would trust to his God, rather than to man.

Since I have been placed in this cell I have read the Scripture, and have found such relief in its blessed words, especially where it speaks of God's love for man; how He loved him, an enemy, a sinner, and sent His Son into the world to save His enemy; how He compels the wretched from the hedges and highways to come into the feast; how any may come, and how He bids them, entreats them. Though it may seem unmanly to accept offers in our adversity which we neglected in prosperity, yet it is even so that with His assistance I will go up and beg forgiveness, and put my trust in the saving blood of Him who died for man. Aye, I pray Him to grant His grace to my mother and sisters and my loved one. If He is with them, who can be against?

What pleasure I take in the hymns I learned in boyhood! They come back to me now in my manhood and in my sorrow, and with God's blessing have wiled away and comforted many a weary and lagging hour.

Dec. 30th. Last evening the doorman bought me a "Book of Common Prayer" for $1.00, and it was and will be a source of great comfort to me. I read over the familiar services and oft-heard hymns, and committed two—"Rock of Ages" and "Sinners turn, why will ye die?"—to memory. There were four accused in the three cells last night. As yet I have heard but one give good advice to another. They all with one accord exhort one another to be good soldiers in warfare *vs.* society, not to give up stolen property; and, above all, not to trust to the detectives, who are their natural and mortal enemies. Such is life!!!

Dec. 31st. The year is gone; begun for me in ——; it sees me, as it dies, a prisoner in New York. To-day I complete my twenty-ninth year. What have I done to make this world any wiser or better? May God bless me in the future; be it in time or eternity. May I be enabled to meet my trials with resignation, patience, and fortitude, as one who serves his country and home and people. The year went out in rain—drizzling rain. Will I see the year 1865 go out? or will I pass away from this world of sin, shame, and suffering?

Jan. 1st, 1865. Sunday, first day of the week and first day of a new year. To-day I enter my thirtieth year of pilgrimage. According to the calculation of my father's family, I am more than half-way down life's stream, even if spared by war and sudden death. But in prying into the future, I can see nothing to induce me to think that my days will be lengthened to that age of fatality, fifty-six. Has my life been so crowded with pleasure or good deeds, that I need desire to prolong it? Alas! no. Though well reared, and surrounded with very many advantages, I have not done any thing to give me particular pleasure; nor, on the other hand, have I been remarkable for the opposite. I am truly thankful that I always stayed with mother and the girls and tried to do my duty by them; that is one consolation at least, and also that I never voluntarily left them. They know not where I am to-day; and every one of them is this day thinking of me. Little do they know where I am. Indeed, I doubt if they have heard any thing definite from me for many a weary month. Oh this war!

This far on life's way I have lived an honest life, defrauding no man. Those blows that I have struck have been against the society of a hostile nation; not against the society of which I am a member by right, or *vs.* mankind generally. To-day the thought has obtruded itself again and again to become an "Ishmael." Your country is ruined, your hopes dashed—make the best bargain for yourself. "Remember the history of the civil wars of France, of England—the examples of Talleyrand, Josephine, &c.; of Shaftesbury, Caermarthen, Marlborough, &c." To-day my hands have no blood on them (unless of man in open battle); may I say so when I die. I saw grandfather and father die; they both took great comfort from the thought that no one could say that they had of malice aforethought injured them. Better the sudden death, or all the loathsome corruption of a lingering life, with honor and a pure conscience, than a long life with all material comforts and the canker-worm of infelt and constant dwelling dishonor; aye, a thousand times. O God, our Creator, Preserver, and Saviour! I pray give me strength to resist temptation, to drive back the thick-coming fancies brooded of sin and dishonor, and to cling to the faith of Jesus, who said, "Do unto others as you would that they should do unto you."

Jan. 2d. Last night was called out, and a search made of my room and my person. The captures consisted of two knives. Poor Grimes! your gift and keepsake was duly declared contraband and confiscated. They gave me two newspapers, which do seem to bear out the statements of Southern loss, &c. Savannah, indeed, is fallen; but its garrison was saved, so that Hardee and Beauregard have an army. And Butler did not take Wilmington, though the fleet did storm long and heavy. Poor Bragg has some laurels at last. Oh that Gen. Lee had 50,000 good fresh veteran reënforcements! But what are these things to me here! I do most earnestly wish that I was in Richmond. Oh for the wings to fly to the uttermost part of the earth!

What would I do without the Bible and Prayer-book, and the faith taught in them, best boon of God, the fount of every blessing? That faith nothing can take away save God.

Exhibit E.

[COPY.]

Confederate States of America, Navy Department,
Richmond, *March 5th*, 1863.

SIR:—You are hereby informed that the President has appointed you an Acting Master in the Navy of the Confederate States. You are requested to signify your acceptance or non-acceptance of this appointment; and should you accept, you will sign before a magistrate the oath of office herewith, and forward the same, with your letter of acceptance, to this Department.

Registered No. ——.

The lowest number takes rank.

(Signed)   S. P. MALLORY,
Secretary of the Navy.

Acting Master JOHN Y. BEALL, of Va., C. S. N.,
Richmond, Va.

[ENDORSED.]

Confederate States of America, Navy Department,
Richmond, 23*d December*, 1864.

I certify that the reverse of this page presents a true copy of the warrant granted to John Y. Beall, as an Acting Master in the Navy of the Confederate States, from the records of this Department.

In testimony whereof I have herewith set my hand and affix the seal of this Department, on the day and year above written.

(Signed)   S. P. MALLORY,
Secretary of the Navy.

Exhibit F.

BY AUTHORITY.—CONFEDERATE STATES OF AMERICA.

Whereas, It has been made known to me that BENNETT G. BURLEY, an Acting Master in the Navy of the Confederate States, is now under arrest in one of the British North American provinces, on an application made by the Government of the United States for the delivery to that Government of the said BENNETT G. BURLEY, under the treaty known as the Extradition Treaty, now in force between the United States and Great Britain; and whereas it has been represented to me that the said demand for the extradition of said BENNETT G. BURLEY is based on the charge that the said BURLEY is a fugitive from justice, accused of having committed the crimes of robbery and piracy in the jurisdiction of the United States; and whereas, it has further been made known to me that the accusations and charges made against the said BENNETT G. BURLEY are based solely on the acts and conduct of said BURLEY, in an enterprise made or attempted in the month of

September last (1864), for the capture of the steamer *Michigan*, an armed vessel of the United States, navigating the lakes on the boundary line between the United States and the said British North American Provinces, and for the release of numerous citizens of the Confederate States, held as prisoners of war by the United States at a certain island called Johnson's Island; and whereas, the said enterprise or expedition for the capture of the said armed steamer *Michigan*, and for the release of the said prisoners on Johnson's Island, was a proper and legitimate belligerent operation, undertaken during the pending public war between the two Confederacies, known respectively as the Confederate States of America and the United States of America, which operation was ordered, directed, and sustained by the authority of the Government of the Confederate States, and confided to its commissioned officers for execution, among which officers is the said BENNETT G. BURLEY;

Now, therefore, I, JEFFERSON DAVIS, President of the Confederate States of America, do hereby declare and make known to all whom it may concern, that the expedition aforesaid, undertaken in the month of September last, for the capture of the armed steamer *Michigan*, a vessel of war of the United States, and for the release of the prisoners of war, citizens of the Confederate States of America, held captive by the United States of America at Johnson's Island, was a belligerent expedition ordered and undertaken under the authority of the Confederate States of America, against the United States of America, and that the Government of the Confederate States of America assumes the responsibility of answering for the acts and conduct of any of its officers engaged in said expedition, and especially of the said BENNETT G. BURLEY, an Acting Master in the navy of the Confederate States.

And I do further make known to all whom it may concern, that in the orders and instructions given to the officers engaged in said expedition, they were specially directed and enjoined to "abstain from violating any of the laws and regulations of the Canadian or British authorities in relation to neutrality," and that the combination necessary to effect the purpose of said expedition "must be made by Confederate soldiers and such assistance as they might (you may) draw from the enemy's country."

In testimony whereof I have signed this manifesto, and directed the same to be sealed with the seal of the Department of State of the Confederate States of America, and to be made public.

Done at the city of Richmond, on the 24th day of December, 1864.

JEFFERSON DAVIS.

By the President,
J. P. BENJAMIN, *Sec. of State.*

Exhibit G.

Address of James T. Brady, Esq., Counsel for the accused.

MR. PRESIDENT AND GENTLEMEN OF THE COMMISSION: Since I had the honor of appearing before this Court on the last day, there has been a publication in all our newspapers relating to the activity and success of a number of our detectives in ferreting out, as is supposed, the perpetrators of the attempt to fire the city of New York. That, of course, you gentlemen have all read, and being gentlemen of intelligence, reading it has made some impression on your mind. In ordinary cases an advocate seeking every advantage for an accused party, lays great stress on the fact that a person called a juror may have had his mind impressed by the publication of a statement affecting him, and it is, as you know, a reason frequently for setting a juror aside; I have never, either as a lawyer or individual, attached much importance to that suggestion. I should be very sorry though, if any man claiming to be intelligent, should read any account of a transaction, and say it did not produce some kind of impression on his mind, and I only allude to it now for the purpose of saying that Captain Beall's name was mixed up in that, with a great many inaccuracies, and so far as there is any hint or suggestion there that he was either connected, or could be connected with that incendiary attempt, it is without foundation. He spurns any such suggestion; and he has spent most of the time since I came into this room in vindicating himself from such an aspersion; and he begs, that if the Court have any idea that he had the least concern in that transaction, he may be put upon his trial for that. He talks like a soldier and like a gentleman, and expresses the most unlimited confidence in the fairness and integrity of this Commission; but he has the natural apprehension that every man would have in like position, that these out-door publications may insensibly affect the mind of some persons—though he feels from the profession, and the dignity and professional honor of the Court, that he is hardly warranted in entertaining that idea, however remotely. I wish to assure him, and to say to the Court, that I have no such fears. And I can say to the Court, what they may have ascertained—what the Government can be informed of if necessary and proper, that Mr. Beall is of highly-respectable origin. His ancestors emigrated many years ago from the north of Ireland. He was a man of considerable property in the South, and he entered into the fight which is now going on from such motives as had impelled men of high intelligence, and men who, however delusively influenced to such an opinion, really think as sincerely as we believe in the sacred cause that we sustain, that they were acting from the most laudable motives. And while I presume that all the gentlemen in this room, like myself, feel that this battle should never cease on our side until we have imposed again the authority and power of our Government over all the territory we ever possessed, and even feel, as I certainly do for one, that when that shall have been accomplished, the power of this Government should be felt in other directions, whenever the justification arises ; yet we would be false to our Maker if we supposed that all the men who fought on the other side were hypocrites and fanatics, or were impelled by such bad motives as impelled men to perpetrate crime. It would be inconsistent with my views of the majesty and justice of the Almighty that he should permit such men, led by such intellects, to act entirely from unreasonable and blind and wicked impulses. That we have justice on our side is undoubtedly in our belief certain. But soldiers, whatever civilians may do, will never look at an enemy like the one we are contending against, as utterly bereft of reason, as utterly inferior to us, and not exactly level with the brutes. The accused has been, as the gentlemen of this Court have learned from his diary, I think, intelligently educated ; and whether it makes for him or against him, he has received sound moral culture. The mother and the sister to whom he so affectionately refers in that diary, have exercised over him—the mother first, and the sister afterwards—those ennobling influences which in the homestead exercise their great power over all of us in childhood and after life. And being a gentleman of education, a graduate of the University of Virginia, he has his own views about this case, and has communicated them to me, and I will present them to you. I have never had the pleasure of addressing, except as a private citizen, any of the honorable members of this Court ; and my friend Major Bolles—I am sure he will permit me to call him so, as he has acted as such toward me—and myself have never been associated or opposed in any matter. And for that reason, at the risk of being considered, for the moment, egotistical, I wish to say to this Court, on the honor of a gentleman, that I never have supposed that Lord Brougham's definition of the duties or right of an advocate was correct. I have never entertained the idea that it proceeds, in the view of refined society, or in the view of any instructed conscience, further than this, that an advocate may fairly present honorably whatever any man who is accused would have a right in truth to say for himself, and no more. With that view of the duty which I am attempting to discharge on this occasion, I present in the first place the prisoner's proposition that this Court has no jurisdiction of the matters which are here being investigated ; that the trial of these offences should take place in a general court-martial, organized according to the well-established principles of the laws of war ; and that a Military Commission, though it may exercise power over the citizens' of the Government which establishes it, cannot, according to the law of war and of nations, take cognizance of the specific accusations presented here. I have never examined this question at all until this trial arose; and I say to you, that the questions involved in this case, except so far as I have derived any knowledge from my general reading as a lawyer, are new to me. Some of them seem to be novel even in reference to the large experience of the Judge Advocate General, whose opinions are contained in the Digest of his decisions recently published.

I find by looking through the history of jurisdiction, especially as to spies, that by an Act of Congress of 1808, it is in terms declared that a person charged as a spy shall be tried by a general court-martial. The Act of the 13th of February, 1862, contains the same provision; but the Act of 1863 provides that persons embraced in the description of spies as there given, may be tried by a court-martial or military commission; and of course it would seem that if it were within the power of Congress to make such a law, there is a specific warrant for trying this party before a military commission on the charge of being a spy. How much further it extends is a little questionable. But there is this peculiarity, to which I must call the attention of the Court. I refer to the Revised United States Army Regulations of 1863, page 541. In the Act of 1863 it is provided in the first Section, that so much of the law of July 17th, 1862, as requires the approval of the President "to carry into execution the sentence of a court-martial, be, and the same is hereby repealed, as far as relates to carrying into execution the sentence of any court-martial against any person convicted as a spy or deserter."

You see, therefore, that unless there is something to modify this, a peculiarity arises from this legislation if a man be tried before a court-martial.

[The Judge Advocate called the attention of the counsel for the accused to the Act of July 2d, 1864, chapter 215, passed at the last session of Congress, which extends the provision to sentences of military commissions as well as court-martials on the trial of spies, guerrillas, &c. Mr. Brady resumed as follows:]

I am very much obliged to you, and I am confident that something has occurred in legislation on that subject, or in the decisions. I believe one of the decisions of the Judge Advocate General was to the effect that in equity, that provision would be extended to the cases of conviction before a military commission. But I had not in my library the Act of the last session; and that being explained to me, I have said all that I wish to present on the subject of jurisdiction, and pass from that to another proposition, and that is, that Capt. Beall in these charges and specifications seems to be treated in two aspects: one as a mere individual, engaged in the perpetration of an offence against society at large; and the other in the character of a military man, offending against the laws of war. If what is here presented against him in the proof shows that he has only committed some offence against general society cognizable in the ordinary courts of judicature, then he would be entitled under the Constitution of the United States to a trial by jury. That right accompanies him as a citizen of the United States, without any reference to what any revolting States may declare; and whatever the South may say or think, we have not given up a single provision of our Constitution in regard to those matters, although we have heard of, and the Government has acted on the idea of the suspension of the habeas corpus, and done other acts incident and proper to a state of war, so that some of the provisions of the Constitution have been to a certain extent interfered with. The Court of course perceives at once that I am correct in saying he is so treated. I will refer to this Digest of the opinions of the Judge Advocate General, at pages 79 and 81. I read first the 11th paragraph:

"Where a military commission was invested by the original order of the general convening it, 'with jurisdiction in all cases civil, criminal, and in equity, usually triable in courts established by law'—held that such a tribunal was not authorized to be created, either by law or usage, and *recommended* that it be ordered by the Secretary of War to be dissolved." Very properly, because in that case it would seem, that in organizing the court the orders grasps all kinds of jurisdiction incident to the ordinary tribunals, and that was an assumption of power which the Government through its proper officers, very properly reprehended. I then read paragraph 16, which is as follows:

"The murder of Union soldiers, for the disloyal and treasonable purpose of resisting the Government in its efforts to suppress the rebellion, is a military offence, quite other than the ordinary offence of murder, cognizable by the criminal courts; and citizens who have been guilty thereof, though in a State where the courts are open, may be brought to trial before a military commission. In such case, the circumstances conferring jurisdiction should be indicated in the charge and distinctly set forth in the specification." That will commend itself to every member of this Court. It is quite possible that a man in the Confederate service, ordinarily engaged as a soldier by his Government —I shall use their phrase of course—might come within our lines and perpetrate a murder as an individual, in a way and under circumstances wholly divested of any relation with his military character, for private gain or personal revenge. The mere fact that he was a Confederate soldier, that he was within our lines, and that he murdered one of our citizens, would not render him amenable either to a court-martial or a military commission, if the circumstances indicated nothing giving it the quality of a military offence. That you very well understand. That is illustrated in this case of murder, where the Court and Judge Advocate must state the special circumstances which give to that murder of Union soldiers the quality and character bringing it within the jurisdiction of a military tribunal.

Now, in the expedition of Lake Erie, with which the accused is connected, and the other attempt on the railroad, offences were committed cognizable by the laws, in one case of Ohio and in the other of New York; punishable by those laws. And if the evidence should establish that the persons engaged in either of those acts were acting irrespective of character as soldiers of the Confederate Government, then we respectfully submit that neither this Court nor a Court-martial would have authority to try the accused. If one of our soldiers should straggle and go into Richmond, or into any of the towns along the path of Sherman's army, and remain there and secrete himself and commit larceny or burglary, he would not be amenable to any court-martial in the South for any such act, as we understand it. And we apply the same principle to the same act perpetrated in our lines by a Confederate soldier.

In regard to the offence of the attempt to throw this railroad train off the track, wholly irrespective of the design avowed, according to the testimony of the witness Anderson, to take possession of the safe and money, we have a statute in New York, passed in 1838, which distinctly makes it an offence to do any such thing in regard to railroad trains, and subjects the offender to five years' imprisonment in the State's Prison, or one year in the penitentiary, according to the judgment and discretion of the court.

The Act of March, 1863, section 30, provides this: "*And be it further enacted*, That in times of war, insurrection, or rebellion, murder, assault and battery with an intent to kill, manslaughter, mayhem, wounding by shooting or stabbing, with an intent to commit murder, robbery, arson, burglary, rape, assault and battery with an intent to commit rape and larceny, shall be punishable by the sentence of a general court-martial or military commission, when committed by persons who are in the military service of the United States, and subject to the articles of war." Congress deemed it necessary thus to provide for the authority of a court-martial to punish our own citizens when in the military service, for the crimes of murder, robbery, &c.

But the accused and myself respectfully submit that the perpetration by a man who happens to be a Confederate soldier, within our territory, of an offence, in the consummation of which he acts not in any military capacity or quality, is not an offence which a court-martial or military commission can take cognizance of. And if you look at this man who is here now, as here amongst us without a uniform, acting as a mere aggressor against general society, the punishment of his offence belongs to the ordinary tribunals and not to this. I will consider that again in connection with the specific charge of his being a guerrilla, where it is supposed that the due authority for taking cognizance of this case will be found. I pass it for the present, having closed what I intended to say on the subject of the tribunal which should investigate this case, and the principles by which they should be governed.

The accused also insists through the medium of his own reason and his reading and reflection, that the charge—particularly the first charge—" violating the laws of war," is too general and vague, and does not conform to the requirements of the law applicable to cases of this character.

When I was first consulted in this case, it was suggested that the objection to the generality of this charge should be made at the outset, and that is the usual course. But I said that so far as that objection was worthy of any consideration, the honorable members of this Court would consider it quite as much in their ultimate action as if the objection was specifically made. And I must say to my client, with your permission, that usually the objection to any thing on account of its generality is not of practical value, because if it be erroneous, it is only informing your adversary to make it more specific. It is of no advantage to the accused; and I hope the accused, in this instance, will feel, as I do, that this Court has acted with the greatest possible courtesy—certainly to me and I think to the accused; and the Judge Advocate has not done any thing in this case not eminently professional and honorable, and I am certain he will do nothing prejudicial to the accused except in such manner as becomes an officer and a gentleman. I lay no stress, therefore, upon this objection as to the generality of the charge, because I don't see that there is any substance in it, except the one that naturally suggests itself to the accused that he might be tried again, and the charge, "Violation of the laws of war," would not show what specific offences were presented against him. I leave this part of the case with just that remark, and come directly to what I understand to be the substance of the two accusations, without reference to the language of the specifications. And we have ourselves met with the charge, in the first place, that he was a spy; and, in the second place, a guerrilla.

This charge of being a spy seems, from the language of these specifications and the tenor of the proof, intended to apply to him during all the time that he was in the condition which, for the present, I shall call *within our lines*, though I presently may have to ask this Honorable Court to inform themselves what that phrase means, as applied to the particular war now being waged between the two sections of our country. What are lines? Now, as to his being a spy, I may deceive myself, but I see no proof whatever to justify that accusation. And if, in what I am now about to say, I shall accidentally bring my mind in conflict with any settled opinions which you gentlemen of the profession of war may have in your own minds, you will be good enough mentally to pardon me and wait until I get through with the demonstration I attempt to offer. And not to appear pedantic, as any man may become, who looks through encyclopædias and dictionaries, and gets the reputation of being learned without the merit; for as the poet has said:

> "Digested learning makes no student pale;
> It takes the eel of science by the tail;"

let me come to the definition of the word *spy*. We know it comes from the French word *espionner*—to observe with the eye.

That definition is certainly not broad enough, because a blind man might be a spy and a very good one. He may roam through the country as a blind beggar, and through his ear receive intelligence to his side of the greatest service.

And, if actual observation with the eye were necessary, Major André was not a spy, for he made no observation within our lines that could be of any possible service. He was not there for that object. He came there to meet Arnold, to get despatches with a view to deliver them to Sir Henry Clinton. He was convicted of being a spy because he was within the enemy's line to receive intelligence, and deliver it to the Commander-in-chief of his own army, that it might be used against the Colonies.

That is a very clear case of being a spy; just as clear as the case of Davis who was convicted the other day, a man who was carrying despatches from Canada to the South, and passing through our lines for the purpose of communicating that intelligence. And I cannot imagine how all this sympathy is wasted upon André, which I am sorry to say has found its way into the excellent work of Phillimore on International Law. It is true that André had on a uniform, but it was covered over with an outer coat. There was an actual concealment of the true character of the man, and he was travelling with a false pass, I may say, from Arnold; and Arnold had the impudence to insist that André should be surrendered to Sir Henry Clinton, because he was travelling under this traitorous pass given by him.

And André the less deserves our sympathy, because one letter of his addressed to Col. Sheldon is in existence, mentioned in Irving's Life of Washington, showing that he intended to take advantage of a flag of truce for the purpose of holding his communications with Arnold. And if any thing on earth known among men, recognized by society, and sustained by humanity, is deserving of veneration, it is a flag of truce—

that Divine aspect of Heaven amidst the grim and bloody horrors of war.

Now the definitions of the term *spy*, which I will take the liberty to mention so as to recall your memories to the nature of the word, are, first, from Webster. He gives three: 1st. "A person sent into an enemy's camp to inspect their works, ascertain their strength and their intentions, to watch their movements, and secretly communicate intelligence to the proper officer. By the laws of war among all civilized nations, a spy is subjected to capital punishment. 2d. A person deputed to watch the conduct of others. 3d. One who watches the conduct of others."

Of course, the first is the only one important in reference to the word *spy* as used in these charges and specifications. Bouvier, in his Law Dictionary, says a spy is "one who goes into a place for the purpose of ascertaining the best way of doing an injury there. The term is mostly applied to an enemy who comes into the camp for the purpose of ascertaining its situation in order to make an attack upon it."

Bailey gives, I think, the best definition of *spy* that I have found anywhere; but of its excellence, of course, you will be the judge. He says a spy is "one who clandestinely searches into the state of places and affairs."

Major General Halleck, in his most valuable treatise on International Law and the Laws of War, at page 406, says this: "Spies are persons who, *in disguise, or under false pretences*, insinuate themselves among the enemy, in order to discover the state of his affairs, to pry into his designs, and then communicate to their employer the information thus obtained. * * * * The term *spy* is frequently applied to persons sent to reconnoitre an enemy's position, his forces, defences, &c., but not in disguise, or under false pretences. Such, however, are not *spies* in the sense in which that term is used in military and international law, nor are persons so employed liable to any more rigorous treatment than ordinary prisoners of war. It is the *disguise*, or *false pretence*, which constitutes the perfidy, and forms the essential element of the crime, which, by the laws of war, is punishable with an ignominious death."

We see, therefore, that irrespective of the Acts of Congress, from the nature and signification of the word *spy*; from the definitions which have been given to it by intelligent writers; from what is said here by the General, who is certainly an excellent authority, there must, to constitute the crime of a spy, be something in the nature of a disguise, and the purpose of it to clandestinely obtain information to communicate it to the enemy. Now, let us see what Congress has said on the subject. I refer to page 502 of the Army Regulations, and this is somewhat interesting to me, whatever it may be to the Court—I mean the character of the legislation on this subject. In 1806, Congress provided: "That in time war all persons not citizens of, or owing allegiance to, the United States of America, who shall be found lurking as spies in or about the fortifications or encampments of the armies of the United States, or any of them, shall suffer death, according to the law and usage of nations, by sentence of a General Court-Marshal."

It related, you see, exclusively to persons not citizens of the United States, and did not owe it allegiance; and no other persons, by the definition of Congress, could be regarded as spies. So matters remained, for we had no occasion to legislate on the subject at all, until the act of 1862 was passed, which provides "that, in time of war or rebellion against the supreme authority of the United States, all persons who shall be found lurking as spies or acting as such, in or about the fortifications, encampments, posts, quarters, or headquarters of the armies of the United States, or any of them, within any part of the United States which has been or may be declared to be in a state of insurrection by proclamation of the President of the United States, shall suffer death by a general court-martial."

That you will perceive is a provision made to reach the case of persons acting as spies in the South, or in such portions of the States, or in such States as were in rebellion; and Congress seems to have considered that special legislation was necessary for that object; and that won't apply to the accused; but, in 1863, the last legislation that I know of on this subject contains the provision: "*And be it further enacted,* That all persons who, in time of war or of rebellion against the supreme authority of the United States, shall be found lurking, or *acting* as *spies* in or about any of the fortifications, posts, quarters, or encampments of any of the armies of the United States, or *elsewhere*, shall be triable by a general court-martial or military commission, and shall, upon conviction, suffer death."

All persons—there is no longer the distinction that they shall not be citizens or owe allegiance to the United States. The term is now large and comprehensive; but they must be lurking or acting as spies in or about the fortifications, camps, &c.; and I would respectfully submit to the Court that the words " or *elsewhere*," only mean elsewhere in reference to something of the same character. They cannot mean any place in the wide world, because, according to that definition, if a man were out in the middle of the prairies on his way, or if he were in any State in the South, if he were near any fortification that we had there, or was away from any fortification, if he were lurking, it would reach him. Therefore it seems that so far as Congress has legislated upon this subject, they only treat as a spy a person who is lurking, acting specifically as a spy, in or near some place where the army is, with a view to detect its movements and inform the enemy; and the question will be whether the prisoner stands in that category. Now, of course I heard when I was a boy, before I had ever looked at a law book, that there was a traditional idea, and it seems to have prevailed to this moment, that the mere fact of an enemy's being found within the lines of an adversary, without a uniform, constitutes the offence of being a *spy*. We find that that is not strictly correct, or else it becomes correct by reason of his appearing without a uniform being equivalent to assuming a disguise.

Well, of course, it is just as much a disguise to take off a dress by which you are ordinarily characterized, as to put on one different from your ordinary garb. That I concede, and it is very plain; but in the case of the accused, there is no proof that he ever had a uniform, that he ever owned one or wore one; and I suppose you, gentleman, know that, as a general thing, if not almost invariably, there is no such thing as a uniform in the South, and has not been for two or three years, except in the general resemblance that their clothes have; and I believe you know that, in almost every case, if I am correctly informed, where an officer of the Confederate Government has been captured by our side, he has not had on any buttons or other insignia to denote his rank or condition. There may have been many cases to the contrary; but if I am correctly informed, General Johnson, when captured by Hancock, had no uniform on. He had a round hat, and was very ordinarily attired. He was found in our lines, and in citizen's dress. Where he got that dress; how long he had worn it; whether he had had any other for the last five years, we know nothing about. But whatever may have been his dress at any time while within our territory, when will this Honourable Court say that the accused was within our lines, which is essential to constitute his being a spy? What are, in a military sense, the lines of the United States Army for the purpose of determining the question of one's being a spy, or any other question? Now, even if I felt so disposed, I have not the capacity to give this Honorable Court any information. That is a matter which military gentlemen understand perfectly, and they must determine for themselves. All of us who have been educated at all have some general idea of it; but when we seek for definitions from the lexicographers, we derive very little assistance. I find Mr. Webster, in his dictionary, only gives one: " A trench or rampart; an extended work in fortification," for which definition he cites Dryden. Now, I respectfully ask you, what are the lines of the United States Army, the being within which, in disguise, would constitute being a spy, if there were nothing to take that character away from the accused party? Do you mean all of the United States not in rebellion? Why any more or less than all the territory that the United States ever occupied or governed? We have never consented to the idea that we have parted with one inch of that territory for any purpose. We claim that the United States exist now as they always did, and exist under the same Constitution as ever, for there is no other Constitution; and whatever moral progress, whatever intellectual progress, we may have made, however far we may have advanced toward any philanthropic or other result, we have had no other Constitution, and we never can have, until we change it in the mode prescribed in the Constitution itself, and by which we have just taken a step toward the abolition of slavery. So that, in a general sense, if the United States now should get into a war with France or England, according to what seems to be claimed here in the case of Capt. Beall, the whole of our territory would be the lines of the United States Army. Is that so? Or has this word *lines* a particular signification in military law and practice more restricted than that? If it have, you can say to one another what it is; and when this Court shall have disposed of its duties in this case, if I have the pleasure of meeting one of you gentlemen, and there is nothing improper in it, I shall ask you to construct a definition which may be of service to me in the future. But I had supposed the word lines had some reference in general parlance to a camp. You may make a city a camp or an entire district, but I don't know that you can make a whole country a camp. I don't know whether Cæsar, Hannibal, or Alexander, in any of their extensive marches, could have established as their camps the whole country through which they went. I don't suppose that General Sherman could claim the whole of the State of Georgia as his camp. All this may be of very little consideration to you, because you know so much more about it than I; but I respectfully submit that the word lines must mean some imaginary or prescribed territory relating to, and directly affected by the government of the army as such; and in that sense I don't see how Beall was within our lines in a military sense, because he happened to be in the State of Ohio taking passage in a steamboat, or up at Niagara in the State of New York; the State of New York never for one moment being subject to any kind of military occupation. I don't see how the State of Ohio or the State of New York could be within our lines. But that proposition I submit to your intelligence and judgment.

But suppose it should appear that the accused was in disguise, or without uniform, and within our lines; what was he here for? Was he here to lurk as a spy? Why, not at all. The evidence not only fails to show that, but it directly establishes that he was not. A man belonging to the Confederate service might come within our lines without his uniform, for a very lawful purpose. He might come to perform an act of humanity; he might come to see a friend or relation, not to speak one word on the subject of war. I think I may say I know the fact that officers of the armies on both sides who have had the acquaintance of ladies before this war have crossed the lines to visit them. And if you could to a certainty prove that a Confederate officer came within our lines, or they could prove that one of our officers went within their lines for a mere social purpose, it instantly divests him of the character of a spy. I will now refer you to the Digest of the opinions of the Judge Advocate General, page 127: "That an officer or soldier of the rebel army coming within our lines disguised in the dress of a citizen, is *primâ facia* evidence of his being a spy. The disguise so assumed strips him of all claim to be treated as a prisoner of war. But such evidence may be rebutted by proof that he had come within our lines to visit his family, and not for the purpose of obtaining information as a spy." And then this is stated: "The spy must be taken in *flagrante delicto*. If he is successful in making his escape, the crime, according to a well-settled principle of law, does not fathom him, and, of course, if subsequently captured in battle, he cannot be tried for it.

"Merely for a citizen to come secretly within our lines from the South, in violation of paragraph 86, of General Order 100, of 1863, does not constitute him a spy. A rebel soldier, cut off in Early's retreat from Maryland, and wandering about in disguise within our lines for more than a month, and seeking for an opportunity to join the rebel army, but not going outside our lines since first entering them: *held* not strictly chargeable as a spy."

Now, on this subject we find that the accused did not come here as a spy, nor for any such purpose. He came on one occasion, if you believe the testimony in this case, to assist in a demonstration for the relief of the prisoners on Johnson's Island; a specific purpose of war if he acted in a military capacity. And in the other case, he was in the State of New York engaged in the capture of a railroad train, so as to get possession of the mails and money in the express safe; and coming for either of those purposes, he did not come to lurk or make himself a spy in any way. And on that subject the Judge Advocate has been good enough to present the letters and diary of this young man to prove his declarations. Now, on the subject of declarations, the law is this, and it has always been the law: If I prove in reference to a man, in any proceeding, civil or criminal, his statements, they must always be taken together; what exculpates you as well as that which proves you guilty. That is a rule of the soundest reason. If you should happen to shoot a man, and another person should arrest you, and should ask, "Who perpetrated this?" and you should say, "I killed that man, but I did it in self-defence," by no law of reason or justice could the first part of that statement be proved against you and the rest reserved. And more than that; when you prove a man's statements or declarations, as they are called technically, they must be taken as true, unless they are in their nature incredible, or unless they are disproved by some other testimony. Now, we have here the letters written by this man, to which I shall refer—written while he has been in custody; and for what he writes, and states, and does, the accused holds himself responsible.

[Mr. Brady read extracts from the three above-mentioned letters, which are in evidence, and from the diary of the accused, which is also in evidence, and proceeded as follows:]

Now, bearing upon this question of whether he was one who intended to engage in the business of being a spy, I invite your attention to this diary, so impressively read by my friend the Judge Advocate, the other day, where the accused declares in regard to himself, that, although he has been imperfect—and which of us has not—that although his life has not been one unvarying progress of what is pure and good, he only reproaches himself as a Christian reproaches himself; as any one of us reproaches himself in the silent watches of the night, when we are apt to suppose ourselves more completely in the presence of our Maker, and we are compelled to acknowledge the weakness, and imperfections, and folly which have disfigured our lives. It is only in this sense he has reproached himself. But he takes credit to himself, and thanks the Lord that he can say: "I never stained my hand with the blood of my fellow man, except in lawful battle; and I cling to my mother and sister, and never left them voluntarily." I cite these things —fortunately in this case—as showing who it is you are trying, and as bearing upon the general probability of this young man, just thirty years of age, having forgotten the principles that he learned at the fireside, and by hereditary transmission from honored and honorable parents—the probability of his doing any thing except what he intended to be, and regarded as honorable warfare, according to the civilized customs of mankind. And I can assure you that there is nothing in that man's nature which does not make it abhorrent to him, if I am a judge of human nature at all, to do any thing than what a misled Virginian would think was just and manly, on the side to which his conscience, conviction, education, and military attainments, led him. I think, therefore, that I am warranted in saying, that the charge of being a spy is not only not sustained, but entirely disproved. He did not come as a spy; he did not lurk as a spy; he sought no information; he obtained none; he communicated none. He was arrested at Niagara on his way to Canada, having, according to his declaration to Mr. Thomas, a witness of the Government, and whose statement the Government must act upon, reached Baltimore after the failure of the expedition on Lake Erie, been provided there with funds, and was making his way to Canada. He was just exactly in the condition of that soldier in Early's army who had been wandering about in our lines in disguise, waiting for an opportunity to return to the rebel force. And that is precisely what this man was engaged in doing, irrespective of the assault upon the railroad train to which I am about to refer. Under those circumstances he was not a spy—he was any thing and every thing but a spy. He was acting under a commission; he was in the service of the rebel Government; he was engaged in carrying on warfare; he was not endeavoring to perpetrate any offence against society. And if he were not acting under a commission or with authority, but was acting upon his own responsibility and from the wicked intent of his own heart for motives of personal malice or gain, he is not amenable to this tribunal, but must answer to the ordinary courts of the State within which the crime was committed.

I now proceed to the second subject—the accusation that he was acting in violation of the law of war as a guerrilla. On that subject the Judge Advocate General says, at page 66:

"The charge of being a guerrilla may be deemed a military offence *per se* like that of 'being a spy,' the character of the guerrilla having become, during the present rebellion, as well understood as that of a spy, and the charge being therefore such an one as could not possibly mislead the accused as to its nature or criminality if proved, or embarrass him in making his plea or defence. The epithet 'guerrilla' has, in fact, became so familiar, that, as in the case of the term 'spy,' its mere annunciation carries with it a legal definition of crime."

I have the pleasure of knowing the Judge Advocate General well. He is a very able lawyer, and perhaps not surpassed for genius and eloquence by any man alive—certainly in forensic efforts there is no man living who, in my judgment, is equal to him; and those who have not heard him, have been deprived of what is a great intellectual treat. I can understand that his intelligence has exhausted that particular subject to which he refers, of the sufficiency of the charge against an accused that he is a guerrilla. But I do not find that he has given his opinion authoritatively on what is the real meaning of that term, nor to what kind of warfare it relates. I shall, therefore, look at other authorities in connection with that subject. Originally, we find from looking to history that an enemy was regarded as a criminal and an outlaw, who had forfeited all his rights, and whose life, liberty, and property were at the mercy of the conqueror. That was softened down from such rugged asperity by the advance of civilization and Christianity, but essentially the principle remains. The soldiers who surrounded Captain Beall on his way to this Court, and unknown to their superior officer, when the opportunity presents itself, murmur out in his hearing words that would denote that he was contemplated by them as a murderer, an outcast, and a villain, have not brought themselves to understand, to contemplate the dreadful fact, that war is nothing but legalized deception, and fraud, and murder. If I slay my fellow-being upon a provocation or insult, if he should assail the reputation of my mother, or offer insult to my sister in my presence, and in a moment of passion I slay him, by the law of the land I am guilty of murder, although the circumstances might recommend me to the clemency of the Court. And yet, if in obedience to the call of my country I go against the phalanx of men who have done me no personal wrong, do not I always gain my military triumph by the massacre of those innocent men? If you march your battalions against the conscripted armies of the South, who suffer but the innocent? while the guilty leaders—the wicked men who set this rebellion on foot, have thus far escaped, and seem destined to escape, whatever may be the issue of the war. Soldiers like you are not to be horrified by the fact that men engaged in a warfare, who treat you, and consider you to be their enemies, take possesion of your steamboats, or obstruct railroads, or endeavor to throw railroad trains off the track. It is very horrible to contemplate, when you look at it through the lens of ordinary society. A man who in times of peace lays obstacles upon the track for the purpose of throwing off a train in which there may be innocent women and children, not to speak of full-grown men, is regarded as a fiend. But has it not been a customary thing in this war, in all these expeditions called raids, for leaders to earn brilliant reputations by among other things tearing up rails, removing them, intercepting and stopping railroad cars, without reference to the question of who happened to be in them? Would a general officer, or any one in command, who sought to interrupt the communication by rail between two of the enemy's posts, let a train pass through or stop it? If he seeks to stop it he must apply to it the means necessary to accomplish it. Before the days of railroads, when soldiers were transported by means of animals attached to some kind of conveyance, did a General engaged in warfare, who wanted to stop the soldiers, whether they were in stage-coaches (if soldiers ever travelled in that manner) or in caravans, ever stop to see how many innocent people would suffer by assailing them with weapons of destruction? Certainly not. It is death, desolation, mutilation, and massacre, that you are permitted to accomplish in war. And you look at it not through the medium of philanthropy, not through the Divine precept that tells you to love your neighbors as yourself, but through the melancholy necessity that characterizes the awful nature of war. You must change your whole intellect and moral nature to look at it as it is, the *ultima ratio regum*—the last necessity of kings.

This being so, legalized war justifying every method, every horrible resource of interrupting communication, where do you draw the line of distinction between the act of one you call a guerrilla and the act of one you call a raider, like Grierson? Where do you make the distinction between the march of Major-General Sherman through the enemy's country, carrying ravage and desolation everywhere, destroying the most peaceable and lawful industry, mills and machinery, and every thing of that nature; where do you draw the line between his march through Georgia and an expedition of twenty men acting under commission who get into any of the States we claim to be in the Union, and commit depredations there? And what difference does it make if they act under commission, if they kill the innocent or the guilty? There are no distinctions of that kind in war. You kill your enemy; you put him *hors de combat* in any way, with some few qualifications that civilization has introduced. You may say it is not allowed to use poisoned weapons, and yet we use Greek fire. You may not poison wells, but you may destroy your enemy's property. Even Cicero, in his oration against Verres, when the question arose whether the sacred things were to be preserved in warfare, said: "No, even sacred things become profane when they belong to an enemy." Now, I don't perceive that this term " guerrilla" has been interpreted so fully as one would seem to think from a hasty glance at the Judge Advocate General's opinion to which I have referred. At the outbreak of this war the Savannah privateers were captured; they were held and tried as pirates. I was one of the counsel for the accused. The jury in the city of New York disagreed. In Philadelphia they convicted some of them; and as the honorable members of this court remember, the Confederate Government proposed retaliation, and took an equal number of our men, their lot being determined by chance, and secured them, to be executed in case death were visited upon any of the privateers; and one of the men who was so held was Major Coggswell, who has just left this room; and for the first time in my life I had an involuntary client, because the life of my friend Coggswell was dependent upon the result. Very soon, however, the Government set aside that idea and gave up the notion that privateers were pirates.

You remember the case of the " Caroline," which occurred in 1840, when the British Government sent its officers within our lines and took a steamboat from one of our citizens and set fire to it, and sent it over the Falls; and you remember the diplomatic controversy that arose, in which it was claimed by England that the principle of *respondeat superior* must apply; that it must be settled by the Government whose agents the perpetrators of that offence were. And although McLeod was tried in New York and escaped by the strange defence of proving himself a liar—by proving that he would not have done the things that he boasted he had done, the idea has not yet been removed that it was something to be settled in the international relations of the two Governments.

We see that there may be transactions which do not seem at the first flush to belong to those of war; and yet on a closer examination of them they prove to come within that description. I refer you to General Halleck's book, at page 306, and I beg your attention to this, as I know you will give it:

"Partisans and guerrilla troops are bands of men self-organized and self-controlled, who carry on war against the public enemy, without being under the direct authority of the State. They have no commissions or enlistments, nor are they enrolled as any part of the military force of the State; and the State is, therefore, only indirectly responsible for their acts. * * * * If authorized and employed by the State, they become a portion of its troops, and the State is as much responsible for their acts as for the acts of any other part of its army. They are no longer partisans and guerrillas in the proper sense of those terms, for they are no longer self-controlled, but carry on hostilities under the direction and authority of the State. * * * It will, however, readily be admitted, that the hostile acts of individuals, or of bands of men, without the authority or sanction of their own Government, are not legitimate acts of war, and, therefore, are punishable according to the nature or character of the offence committed."

If that be so, you cannot convict any man as a guerrilla who holds a commission in the service of the Confederate government, and perpetrates any act of war in that capacity. He is not self-organized with his command, nor self-controlled. He is acting under authority of our foe, and he is regarded as under so much protection as belongs to the law of war. If he has a commission, and do any thing which no man may do belonging to the army under any circumstances whatever, and commits offences which military courts have cognizance of, they will take jurisdiction and award the punishment he deserves.

You will find that in this case Captain Beall was acting as an officer of the Confederate government, either in command himself of Confederate soldiers, or under the command of some Confederate officer, as in the attempt on the railroad where Colonel Martin of the Confederate service was in command. Commissioned officers of the Confederate government engaged in depredations for the purposes of war within our territory, are not guerrillas within this definition of General Halleck, or any definition recognized in any book that I have had occasion to refer to. So far as that definition and the like is concerned, that it is ratified by this Government, is shown from this proclamation of Jefferson

Davis, referred to in specific terms, showing that it was done by authority of the Government. Now permit me, in this connection, to refer you, Mr. Judge Advocate, to Phillimore on International Law, 3d volume, p. 137:

"If the unauthorized subject carry on war, or make captures, it may be an offence against the sovereignty of his *own* nation, but it is not a violation of international law.

"The legal position that no subject can lawfully commit hostilities, or capture property of an enemy, when his sovereign has either expressly or constructively prohibited it, is unquestionable. But it appears to be equally unquestionable, that the sovereign may retractively ratify and validate the authorized act of his subject." He says on page 145: "Guerrillas are bands of marauders, acting without the authority of the sovereign or the order of the military commander. A class which, of course, does not include volunteer corps, which have been permitted to attach themselves to the army, and which act under the commands of the general of the army."

So that a guerrilla must be a marauder, self-controlled, not acting by the authority of his Government, without a commission—a mere self-willed and self-moving depredator. The question is, whether there is any proof of any such character in regard to Capt. Beall. As to the transaction on Lake Erie, I accept all the proof which has been given by the Government. It was an expedition to take possession of that steamboat, at a distance of some six miles from Johnson's Island, to *run down the United States armed steamer Michigan*, then lying at about the distance of a mile from Johnson's Island, and thus give the prisoners on Johnson's Island an opportunity to escape.

[The Judge Advocate said there was no evidence to prove that the purpose was to run down the *Michigan*.]

Mr. Brady resumed. Oh yes! you have proved the declarations of the parties engaged in it on board the boat, by Mr. Ashley. Ashley states expressly that that was the purpose.

[The Court said that the witness said the object was stated to be to capture the *Michigan*.] Mr. Brady again resumed.

That was the purpose of the armed expedition of Confederate soldiers or officers, to take possession of, or capture the *Michigan*, and thus aid to release the prisoners on Johnson's Island. That I call a military expedition; and that I call an expedition which being carried on by men under commission from the Confederate government, is legalized warfare and not the conduct of guerrillas. That, however, must be submitted to your judgment.

Now, what was undertaken at Niagara is proved here by no witness except Anderson. What the accused said to Mr. Thomas, within the rule that I have already announced, that the whole must be taken together and all believed unless it conflicts with other proofs, has no relation to any such thing as this charge. When Capt. Beall was arrested by him, the Captain asked him for what he was arrested, and Thomas said in substance—I don't profess to give the very words— "You know as well as I do."

And then it was stated that he was arrested as an escaped rebel prisoner; and Beall said, "From Point Lookout?" "Yes." "Well," says he, "I confess that I am an escaped prisoner from Point Lookout."

The records of this Government show, I presume, and therefore I am warranted in alluding to the fact, that Capt. Beall was a prisoner, and at Point Lookout, was taken by our forces and exchanged. In his conversation with Thomas he was acting the part of human nature. He wanted to be released if possible. He got the officer to suggest that he was an escaped prisoner; a thing involving no kind of turpitude or wrong, for every prisoner is entitled to escape, civil or criminal. It is the right of every man in society to escape the consequences of his actions; it is the right of society to punish him. But what is the proof? He did not say any thing to him except what I have already narrated. Now, who is Anderson? He is an accomplice. And what is the law as to accomplices? They are competent witnesses. They are often employed from the necessity of public justice. Their testimony, as an old writer says, is tolerated rather than approved. The act of turning traitor to your associate involves what we have regarded from boyhood as the meanest kind of perfidy. And although upon his testimony alone you can convict a party, it is always stated, and it is stated by McArthur on Court-Martials, that he must be corroborated in something tending directly to implicate him. There is the only proof. Now, what was the object of the capture of the express train? There is no person from the railroad to testify in regard to it. We don't know what happened to that train. Somebody went back with lights. We don't know whether any person was injured or not. Certainly according to Anderson's testimony there was no attempt made to take possession of any thing on board. I have not gone into any minutiæ of the testimony; it is not necessary. I shall not follow the wanderings of the statements made by Weston and Hays, who come from the station-house, or as to the details of what was in this carpet-bag, holding it to be entirely immaterial who owned it. Anderson said it belonged to the accused, and the accused said it did not. There were candles. They said they were serviceable when they could not get any other light. There was a bottle of laudanum in the pocket of the accused, which he said was for the toothache. Whether he had the toothache, or intended to poison himself, does not concern us. He had a right to poison himself, except as between Capt. Beall and his Maker, or Capt. Beall and his Government; but it is wholly immaterial what that was for. And then as to the proof which my friend deemed it proper and necessary to give, to which I made no objection, emanating from this Hays, as to what occurred in the station-house; at the very worst, if Hays reported it accurately, it was an attempt to escape. What would either of you gentlemen do if you were captured by the enemy? Get away if you could. I know I was very much rejoiced when my friend, General Franklin, made his escape so adroitly. And whether the accused did or not offer $1,000 to this man, whom he immediately took into his confidence without any reason for bestowing that confidence; whether this man is correct in saying Capt. Beall, when he would not tell him his name, asked him to take his word for $1,000; all this does not bear upon this case. Now this escape, which in the law books is sometimes called flight, is sometimes given in evidence as a circumstance tending to fix crime. If a man should fall in the street, and should be discovered to be dead, and two or three others run away, and there are circumstances tending to prove that they murdered him, the fact that they run away is an item of evidence against them; but only an item of evidence. But in warfare if a man is taken prisoner and afterwards escapes, his escape is sometimes the most poetical transaction in his life; and his daring in getting away entitles him to as much glory as courage on the battle-field. We read it in romance and poetry, and it stirs our hearts as much as any thing in the record of battles.

Therefore, I think, we have two distinct questions here, and only two: Is the accused proved to be a spy? And is he found to be a guerrilla? What proof is there for the purpose of establishing these charges? In the one case we say he was shown to be within our lines, if within our lines at all, not for the purpose of acting as a spy, but for other developed and proved objects inconsistent with his being a spy. In the other case it appears that he was not a guerrilla because he was a commissioned officer in the Confederate service, acting under authority of that government during war, in connection with other military men, for an act of war. If so, then he is not amenable to this jurisdiction. If I were before a tribunal who had not been accustomed to look at war with its grim visage, with the eye of educated intelligence, I should apprehend that the natural detestation of violence and bloodshed and wrong would pursue this man. But however wrong the South may be—however dismal its records may remain in the contemplation of those who have the ideas of patriotism that reside in our minds—yet not one of you, gentlemen, would even be willing to acknowledge to any foreigner, hating our institutions, that you did not still cling to the South in this struggle, wrong and dreadful as it has been, and award them the attributes of intelligence and courage never before perhaps equalled, and certainly never surpassed, in the annals of the human race.

Bad as their acts may be in our contemplation, have you any doubt that in the conscience of that man, in the judgement of his mother, in the lessons he received from his father, he has what we may think the misfortune of believing himself right?

That mother and those sisters who are watching the course of this trial with their hearts bleeding every instant to think of the condition of the son and brother, who would not care if he should be shot down in one hour in open battle, contending for the principles which they, like him, have approved; if he were borne back to that mother like the Spartan son upon a shield, she would look at his corpse and feel that it was honored by the death he received. But she would be humiliated to the last degree if she supposed that he had departed from the legitimate sphere of battle, and turned his eyes away from the teachings of civilization, and become a lawless depredator, and deserving and suffering ignominious death.

I leave his fate in your hands. I have endeavored to avoid any attempt to address to you any thing but what becomes the sober reason of intelligent men. There are occasions when the advocate may attempt, if he possesses any endowment of that nature, what is commonly called eloquence, what is known as oratory. But I never consider that in a court like this any address of that nature is appropriate in any sense or degree. This is a thing to be reasoned upon. You will view it through the medium of reason with which the Almighty has endowed you. And I think I may say to my client, that whatever conclusions this Court reaches, it will be that of honorable and intelligent gentlemen, who would convict him, if at all, not because he is a southern officer, but because it is the imperious necessity of the law that they deem to be sufficient.

Exhibit H.

Address of the Judge Advocate, Major John A. Bolles A. D. C.

Mr. President and Gentlemen of the Commission: It would be entirely improper, if it were at all possible, for me to imitate the example and follow the course of the eloquent counsel for the accused. He has a right to be eloquent. He could not help being so even if it were wrongful. I have no such right. He is the *advocate*, I am the *Judge* Advocate. It is my pleasant duty to represent, not one side but both sides of the case; absolute and entire justice; the law as it is, and as it affects the case; the facts as they are, and as they affect the

Government and the accused. It is the duty of the advocate for the accused to seek for his acquittal. It is never the duty of the Judge Advocate to seek for the conviction of the accused; but simply to take care that the facts and the law are spread before the Court and that strict justice be done.

In order that justice may be done in this case, I shall, before proceeding to the body of my address, ask the attention of the Court to one or two preliminary observations suggested by the remarks of the counsel for the accused.

No reference has been made by the prosecution, and none will be made, to any supposed connection of the accused with the November attempt to destroy the city of New York by fire, or with any other matter which is not described in the charges and specifications on which he is tried. The Court cannot, and would not, go beyond the case thus presented, and the evidence adduced by the prosecution.

Allusion has been made in the argument, but I must remind the Court that there is no fact in evidence to warrant any allusion, to the wealth, family, ancestry, and university education of the accused. These are matters quite outside of the case, and have nothing to do with the real inquiry before this tribunal.

Something was said of the accused, as appearing by government records, to have been at some time a prisoner of war at Point Lookout. But no such record is shown. The only evidence in the case that connects him with Point Lookout, is his false statement to policeman Thomas in December, that he had escaped a few days before from that place, in company with Anderson: whereas we prove him to have been at large in September, and to have been passing to and from Canada during the week of his arrest.

It has been argued to you that the accused is honorable, devout, and of tender conscience; and appeals are made to his diary for proofs. What *shall* we, what *must* we, think of *his* conscience who within a fortnight of that atrocious attempt upon the railroad, could devoutly thank God, as he does in that diary, that he has never committed any outcrying sin.

You are asked to show some forbearance toward him on account of his hearty and conscientious belief that the cause in which he has been engaged, the rebel cause, is a righteous and just cause. But on page 11 of that diary, he states amongst his "consolations," that he never, of his own accord, left the home circle of his mother and sisters,—"I never voluntarily left them." Such is his real relation, involuntary, to the rebel service. I cannot regard him, therefore, as a firm believer in the justice of the insurgent cause.

Two papers have been put in evidence by the accused without objection on my part: his letter of appointment as master's mate in the rebel navy, and the "manifesto" of Mr. Davis in regard to Burley and the Lake Erie expedition. I was willing to admit that Beall was a rebel officer, and that all he did was authorized by Mr. Davis; because, in my view of the case, all that was done by the accused, being in violation of the law of war, no commission, command, or manifesto could justify his acts. A soldier is bound to obey the lawful commands of his superior officer. Our 9th article of war punishes him for disobedience to such commands, but none other. His superior officer cannot require or compel any soldier to act as a spy, or as an assassin. If, then, such unlawful command be given and obeyed, its only effect is to prove that both he who gave and he who obeyed the command are criminals, and deserve to be gibbeted together. When did a spy ever seek to justify himself by pleading the command of his general? How can the manifesto of the arch-rebel screen any of his subordinates who has trampled under foot that law of war—for war hath its laws no less than peace—which is binding upon all alike, from the rebel president to the rebel raider?

In this connection I will read some extracts from the opinions of the Chief Justice of the Canadian Court of Queen's Bench and of his associates, in the case of Burley, who was concerned, with the accused, in the seizure and plunder of the Lake Erie steamboats. The Chief Justice said: "But, conceding that there is evidence that the prisoner was an officer in the Confederate service, and that he had the sanction of those who employed him to endeavor to capture the *Michigan*, and to release the prisoners on Johnson's Island, the manifesto put forward as a shield to protect the prisoner from personal responsibility does not extend to what he has actually done; nay, more, it absolutely prohibits a violation of neutral territory or of any rights of neutrals. The prisoner, however, according to the testimony, was a leader in an expedition embarked surreptitiously from a neutral territory; his followers, with their weapons, found him within that territory, and proceeded thence to prosecute their enterprise, whatever it was, into the territory of the United States. Thus assuming their intentions to have been what was professed, they deprived the expedition of the character of lawful hostility, and the very commencement of their enterprise was a violation of neutral territory and contrary to the letter and spirit of the manifesto produced."

In the same case Judge Haggerty observed, that "Had this prisoner been arrested on the wharf in Detroit, as he stepped on the *Philo Parsons*, and avowed and proved his character of a Confederate officer, he would have been in imminent danger of the martial rule applicable to a disguised enemy. Had he been secretly joined there by twenty or thirty persons starting over from the neutral shores of Canada, and then by a sudden assault destroyed some national property, or seized a vessel lying at the wharf and taken the money from the unarmed crew, I think they would, if captured in the act, have great difficulty in maintaining their right to be treated as prisoners of war, with no further responsibility.

"In the Russian war, I think we should hardly have allowed such a mild character to a like number of Russians coming over stealthily from the friendly shores of Detroit to burn, slay, and plunder in Windsor.

"All the prisoner's conduct, while within our jurisdiction during this affair, repels the idea of legitimate warfare. A British subject, without the Queen's license and against her proclamation, in the service of one of the belligerents, acting in concert with persons leaving her ports on the false pretence of peaceful passengers, to wage war on a friendly power—no act of his raises any presumption in favor of his being in good faith a soldier or sailor waging war with his enemy."

Mr. Justice WILSON made use of the following language:

"The evidence returned to us shows, *primâ facie*, that the prisoner committed a robbery in the State of Ohio, one of the United States. But it is answered, first, that the prisoner held a commission as Acting Master in the navy of the Confederate States. The holding of this or any other commission, does not authorize him, *mero motu*, to wage warfare from a neutral territory on the unoffending and non-belligerent subjects of the country at war with the nation whose commission he holds. He says he seized the *Philo Parsons* as an act of war, with intent to liberate the prisoners on Johnson's Island; but for this act he produces no order of any superior officer, and the evidence does not show that he had any such order. He says this robbery was at worst an excess of a belligerent right, which was merged in the principal act. Now, what was the principal act of war performed? Under the pretence of being a passenger, he went on board a freight and passenger steamboat at Detroit. As a favor, he requested the master to touch at Sandwich, a British port, to take in three persons as passengers, which was done. The boat proceeded on its regular voyage to Amherstburgh, a town in this Province, near the mouth of the Detroit River, about fourteen miles below Sandwich. Here about twenty men, dressed in the ordinary attire of the farming people of the United States, with one rough trunk, tied round with a cord, and no other baggage, supposed to be citizens of the United States returning to their homes after an absence to escape the draft for the recruiting of the army of the United States, came on board the steamer. The prisoner and his three fellow-passengers affect no knowledge of the last twenty. The course of the vessel to Sandusky, from the mouth of the river, is southeast. She had to pass a number of islands. The northerly are British, the southerly American. The boundary line of this Province was north of the Bass Islands, and thence between Pele Island and Sandusky Island. Johnson's Island is said to be fourteen miles from the Middle Bass Island, and two miles from Sandusky. Nothing occurred to excite suspicion, or cause alarm, until the boat was clearly within the territory of the United States. Suddenly, the prisoner presented a revolver at Ashley, and drove him, at peril of his life, into the ladies' cabin. Beall, one of his confederates, overcame the mate in a similar manner. The other twenty, more or less, rushed to their trunk, armed themselves with revolvers and hatchets which it contained, acted under the orders of Beall and the prisoner, and the boat became at once under their control. So far, neither of the leaders declares his reason for this proceeding. It was rumored that their object was to liberate the prisoners at Johnson's Island. After some hours, the boat landed at the Middle Bass Island, having taken possession of a small steamboat, the *Island Queen*. At this island, just before Ashley was put on shore, Beall and the prisoner, with revolvers to enforce the command, demanded his money. After getting what was in his drawer, the prisoner insists he has more, and Ashley took from his waistcoat pocket a roll of bills, about $90 he supposes, which the prisoner and Beall share between them. These proceedings, so mean in their inception, and so ignoble in their development and termination, we are asked to consider as acts of war, and to accord to the prisoner belligerent rights. What is there in all this which constitutes the act of war? If the object were to release the prisoners, from all that appears they never were nearer than fourteen miles to Johnson's Island. Was the seizure of this unarmed boat *per se* an act of war? for it has been argued that the robbery was merged in the higher act. The seizure of the boat, for whatever purpose, was one thing, the robbery of Ashley quite another, and in no way that we see, in furtherance of the design now insisted upon, necessary for its accomplishment. But is not the *bona fides* of the enterprise matter of defence which a jury ought to try. Such a trial can only be had where the offence was committed, and we cannot doubt but that justice will be fairly administered.

"Then we are told that although the prisoner has no orders to show authorizing what he did, he has the manifesto of the President of the Confederate States, avowing the act and assuming it, and therefore he is not subject to this charge at all. We accord to that Confederacy the rights of a belligerent, as the United States has done from the day it treated the soldiers of the revolted States as prisoners of war; but there is an obvious distinction between an order to do a belligerent act and the recognition and avowal of such an act after it has been done. The one is an act of war, the other an act of an established government. The one is consistent with what Great Britain acknowledges, the other is not. For as judicially to give effect to the avowal and adoption of this act would be to recognize the existence of the nationality of the Confederate States, which at present our Government refuses to acknowledge.

"Giving for the moment this manifesto its full force, it distinctly disclaims all breaches of neutrality; but it is clear that this expedition took its departure and shipped its arms from our port. But does it assume the responsibility of this seizure and all that was done upon it throughout? If not, it is neither justification nor excuse. I see no authority for the doing of the act, and as an assumption of what was done, therefore, the whole justification fails.

"The attitude of the United States towards us is no concern of ours. Sitting here, whatever they do, while peace exists and this treaty is in force, we are bound to give it effect. We can look with no favor on treachery and fraud, we cannot countenance warfare to be carried on except on the principles of modern civilization. We must not permit, with the sanction of law, our neutral rights to be invaded, our territory made the base of warlike operations, or the refuge from flagrant crimes. Peace is the rule, war the exception of modern times; equivocal acts must be taken most strongly against those who, under pretence of war, commit them. For these reasons I think the prisoner must be remanded on the warrant of the learned Recorder."

Mr. Davis' manifesto in terms forbids all violations of neutral rights, and proposes to ratify only "a proper and legitimate belligerent operation," to wit, the capture of the United States armed steamer *Michigan*, and the release of rebel prisoners at Johnston's Island.

But whatever had been its language, the manifesto could not have justified any violation of the laws of war committed for the sake of accomplishing "a proper and legitimate belligerent operation," such as robbing, stealing, and plundering in disguise; and, as matter of fact, the acts of the accused had no reference to that "operation," not one particle of proof is in the case that any design was formed, or effort made, by the plunderers of the *Philo Parsons* and *Island Queen* to effect that "operation."

You have been asked to reject as unworthy of credit the testimony of George Anderson, in regard to the outrage near Buffalo, because he was an accomplice; and it has been said that the laws regard such evidence with suspicion. There is no arbitrary rule of law on this subject. According to *Benet's Military Law*, pp. 242, 243, you are at liberty to believe or disbelief the testimony of an accomplice according to your own convictions; and upon his testimony, with or without corroboration, you may convict the accused.

The rule of law is equally reasonable in regard to the admissions of the accused, oral or written. If the prosecution puts in a part, it must put in the whole; but when such evidence is actually before you—so says *Benet*, p. 264—it rests with you to either believe or disbelieve either the whole or a part. If, then, you look at the letter of the accused to Mr. Lucas, and find that it describes the accused as an officer in the rebel navy, you may believe it; and if you find it asserting " you know that I am not a guerrillero or a spy," you may believe, or disbelieve that the accused so thinks. But you will never commit the error of supposing that what he asserts on that point is any thing more than his opinion; and upon the same facts which led the accused to that mistaken opinion, you may be compelled by the law and the evidence to find him guilty.

At this stage of the case, as well as at any time, I may answer the remarks of the learned counsel upon the legitimate scope and meaning of the phrase " within our lines." He has quoted an Act of Congress, which, as he thinks, and thinks correctly, punishes spies that are found in the insurgent States, and he has also referred to the later Act which punishes them wherever found; an Act into which the word " elsewhere " was introduced for the purpose of covering all possible cases; and yet he is anxious to have your definition of the words " within our lines." Those words do not appear in this case in charge, specification, or evidence. But there can be no doubt of their meaning in the military mind. Every man is within our lines who enters a loyal State by sea or land, with hostile purposes. Any rebel emissary who has first violated the rights of Canadian neutrality, and then in the guise of a peaceful citizen crossed into our territory, along the whole northern frontier of which are military posts and garrisons, is within our lines; and if he be a rebel officer or soldier, the law pronounces him to be a spy; and unless he can prove that he is not, he will be hung as a spy just as certainly as he is caught and brought to trial.—*Judge Advocate Holt's Digest*, p. 127.

" Within our lines," means any spot within the loyal States where an enemy could do us a mischief, be it the Lake Shore Railroad, where the accused attempted his last enterprise, or the city of New York, in which the November incendiaries endeavored to destroy the commercial metropolis of the country, or Boston or Portland Harbor, into which rebel pirates or privateers might seek entrance, or a traitor spy might try to pilot them. There is no shore or border so remote that it is not now within our lines, and lines that bristle everywhere with bayonets, and frown everywhere with forts and cannon. The phrase "within our lines" is as comprehensive as is the word "elsewhere" in the Act of Congress of March 3, 1863, sec. 38, as given on page 542 of the Revised Army Regulation, which provides that "All persons who in time of war or of rebellion against the supreme authority of the United States, shall be found lurking, or *acting* as spies, in or about any of the fortifications, posts, quarters, or encampments of any of the armies of the United States or *elsewhere*, shall be triable by a general court-martial, or military commission, and shall, upon conviction, suffer death."

The section thus quoted, I beg leave to say, shows that a spy, whoever he may be, and wherever found within the broad limits of the United States, "lurking or acting," is amenable to a military commission like the Court which I now have the honor to address, as well as to a court-martial; and thus I furnish an answer to that question of jurisdiction which was raised by the accused, and which his counsel suggested in the beginning of his address as the first proposition of his client's, and not as his own.

There can be no doubt upon this question of jurisdiction. It is true, as was decided by the Judge Advocate General on p. 79 of *Holt's Digest*, cited by Mr. Brady, that a military commission cannot lawfully be clothed with power "in all cases civil and criminal, and in equity."

But the same authority, on the same page, has decided that "many offences which in time of peace are civil offences, become in time of war military offences, and are to be tried by a military tribunal, even in places where civil tribunals exist."

Major General Halleck, who is himself, as the counsel for the accused admits, of great authority in matters of public law, proclaimed the same doctrine in his celebrated Missouri Order, No. 1, quoted by *Benet*, p. 15.

Will the Court permit me here to answer the claim set up by the accused to be tried by a jury for the crimes now charged against him in connection with the seizure of the steamboats and the attempt upon the train of cars? It is true that if these enormities had been committed in time of peace, or by ordinary citizens, rogues, and desperadoes, they would have been mere municipal or civil offences, and the perpetrators would be amenable to the civil courts and entitled to the trial by jury. But the accused is not prosecuted for a civil offence. He is, by the theory of this case, a military offender, a violator of the law of war.

Mr. Brady himself admits, and quotes *Holt's Digest*, p. 79, par. 16, to show that murder, which is a civil offence under ordinary circumstances, may and does, in time of war, when committed for disloyal and treasonable purposes, become a military offence, and may then be tried by a military court, without the interposition of a jury. In time of war, the offender being a rebel officer in disguise, the question of intent, the *quo animo*, is very easily determined. In this case it is very clear that personal advantage was not the motive that led to the seizure of the steamboats, or the attempt on the railroad. To destroy the commerce of the lakes was one of the objects avowed by the raiding party on Lake Erie; to inflict great injury upon great numbers of their Yankee enemies, and not the crazy expectation that a gang of five rebels could overcome and plunder a thousand passengers, was the purpose of the railroad attack.

The acts charged and specified being military offences are triable by a military court, and the accused has no constitutional right to a jury trial.

"The amendment of the Constitution," says the Judge Advocate General (*Digest*, p. 79, 80, sec. 18), "which gives the right of trial by jury to persons held to answer for capital or otherwise infamous crimes—except when arising in the land or naval forces—is often referred to as conclusive against the jurisdiction of military courts, over such offences when committed by citizens. But, though the letter of the article would give force to such an argument, yet in construing the different parts of the Constitution together, such a literal interpretation of the amendment must be held to give way before the necessity for an efficient exercise of the *war powers* which is vested in Congress by that instrument."

The Judge Advocate General further says: "A striking illustration of the recognition of this principle by the legislation of the country since an early period of our history is furnished by the 57th Article of War, in the fact that it has, from the beginning, rendered amenable to trial by court-martial for certain offences" (holding correspondence with or giving intelligence to the enemy), "not only military persons, but all persons whatsoever."

I will add, that by the act of Congress of 1806 in regard to *spies*, the same jurisdiction of courts-martial was extended to that class of offenders, that they might suffer death "according to the law and usage of nations."

If *citizens* may thus be subjected to trial by such courts, *à fortiori*, may *enemies* and armed rebels be deprived of the trial by jury.

Pending a war like this, not less than in all ordinary wars, that branch of the law of nations of which Congress speaks in the act of 1806, already quoted, as "the law and usage of nations" in regard to spies, *i. e.*, "the law of war;" that law of war exists and takes effect everywhere within the territory of the belligerents, and everywhere by the instrumentality of military tribunals, and without a jury, punishes every offence against natural right and justice which is committed by soldiers or citizens, for disloyal and treasonable purposes.

The accused, not his counsel, is of the opinion, as Mr. Brady informs us, that the 1st charge does not set forth with sufficient particularity the offence alleged against him. By the well-settled rule of law, the charge is always thus brief and general.

The Judge Advocate General (*Digest*, p. 66) has decided that the charge of "being a guerrilla" is sufficient. It is in the specification which follows the charge, that the circumstances constituting the offence, and describing its perpetration, are to be fully and clearly set forth.

DeHart, p. 145. *Benet*, p. 52.

Neither the accused nor his counsel can complain that the specifications under the 1st charge are not sufficiently explicit.

I come now, Mr. President, to the inquiry, what are the true legal character and definition of the offences with which the accused stands charged?

 I. What is it, in law, to be a spy, and do the facts proved come up to the legal requirements?

 II. What is it, in law, to carry on irregular warfare, and has the accused been found guilty of this?

I. The learned counsel for the accused is dissatisfied with every definition of a spy that is comprehensive enough to cover the case on trial; and is a little inconsistent in the matter.

Bouvier, in his Law Dictionary, defines a spy to be "*one who goes into a place for the purpose of ascertaining the best way of doing an injury there.*"

Why is not the counsel for the accused content with that?

The accused was an enemy, who came with hostile intent into both Ohio and New York, to ascertain the best way of injuring their peaceable and unsuspecting inhabitants.

Bailey, in his dictionary, presents a definition which almost seems to satisfy the counsel for the accused. According to that venerable lexicographer a spy is one who "clandestinely searches into the state of places and affairs."

The accused came aboard the *Philo Parsons* clandestinely, with the heart and hate of an enemy, but in the dress and with the profession of a friend; so did he clandestinely enter the *Island Queen;* so did he clandestinely visit Buffalo. Deception, disguise, concealment, falsehood, stamp their guilty image and superscription on all his acts, and on all his declarations.

His dress belies and disguises his real character. If André in uniform was rightly held to be in disguise because of his citizen's overcoat, is Beall not disguised when clad as a citizen throughout, from hat or cap to boots?

His story to officer Thomas was a tissue of falsehoods, for he denied his real name and assumed another; he asserted that he was in the rebel infantry, and not in any other branch of the service, when he *was a naval*, and was *not* a *military* officer; his account of his recent escape with Anderson from Point Lookout, and all its details, was untrue.

Do I say that his dress disguises his real character? It did so at the time of his coming within our lines; but now every disguise is a proof, an exposure, a demonstration, of his genuine character, because he is a spy.

The counsel for the accused believes that Major André was a spy. He also believes that Davis, whose case I do not remember, was properly held to be a spy. According to Mr. Brady's statement, Davis was a rebel officer who was on his way from Canada to the South, carrying despatches, and proceeding without delay through the intervening loyal States, holding communication with no one on his way. According to this admission the true definition of spy includes a class of men who come within the limits of the loyal States from a neutral and friendly territory, not to obtain information, but simply to cross our territory as errand boys, carrying papers which contain information.

Is the learned counsel quite consistent, then, when he goes on to quote as entirely satisfactory to him, Maj. Gen. Halleck's definition of a spy; a definition which requires that the spy should have come within our limits not only to *make* discoveries, but "to *communicate* to their employers the information thus obtained"?

This definition does not cover the case of Davis; nor does it cover the case of those who come of their own accord and have no employer; nor of those who are directed, or are determined, to act on the information they gather, instead of communicating it to any one.

Gen. Halleck himself very properly says, that "it is the disguise or false pretence which constitutes the perfidy and *forms the essential element of the crime.*"

It is very clearly immaterial whether the spy comes as principal or agent, to get information for his own guidance or that of others, or whether the information is to be communicated, or to be retained and acted on without communication or consultation; and the true definition of a spy would include any man who comes in disguise, or clandestinely, into his enemy's territory, to obtain and use, or to obtain and transmit information with hostile intent; or who, being within that territory, treacherously seeks information to be used by himself or others for hostile purposes.

In the General Orders of the War Department, No. 100 (April 24, 1863), paragraph 88, it is said that "a spy is a person who secretly, in disguise or under false pretences, seeks information with the intention of communicating it to the enemy." If to this definition had been added the words "*or of using it as an enemy*," it would, I think, have been exact and all comprehensive.

But why linger and dwell in dictionaries and definitions, when, so far as this case is concerned, the legal character of the accused as a spy is settled by authority beyond all question?

The learned Dr. Lieber, in his letter on Guerrilla parties, thus states the law:

"*A person proved to be a regular soldier of the enemy's army, found in citizen's dress, within the lines of the captor, is universally dealt with as a spy.*"

The learned Judge Advocate General, at the head of our Bureau of Military Justice, has again and again decided that *the fact that "an officer or soldier of the rebel army comes within our lines disguised in the dress of a citizen, is* PRIMA FACIA *evidence of his being a spy,*" and that "*the disguise so assumed strips him of all claim to be treated as a prisoner of war.*" (*Digest*, p. 127.)

It is true, as the Judge Advocate further says: "that such evidence may be rebutted by proof that he had come within the lines to visit his family, and not for the purpose of obtaining information as a spy." (*Digest*, p. 127.)

"It is also true, that if the spy succeeds in making his escape the crime does not follow him; and if he be subsequently captured *in battle*, he cannot be tried for it." (*Digest*, p. 127.)

2. The second branch of this first inquiry is now to be considered, viz.: what are the facts proved to which those rules of law are to be applied?

It is proved and admitted that the accused was in the military and naval service of the rebel authorities. He produces his warrant as Master's Mate in the navy; he told officer Thomas that he was an infantry officer; his counsel contends that in the railroad enterprise he was serving under Col. Martin.

It is proved, in the second place, that he came three several times, in the disguise of a citizen, from Canada to Ohio and New York; *first*, as a passenger in the steamer *Philo Parsons; next*, as a railroad operator, when the brave party of four, Martin, Headley, Beall, and Anderson, attempted in vain to lift a rail from the track; and *finally*, when that heroic band, enlarged by one new recruit, and refreshed by two nights of sleep at Port Colborn, returned upon their chivalric errand, and attacked the Dunkirk train.

If, as the counsel for the accused argues, the statement of Anderson the accomplice in this railroad enterprise, is not to be believed—and all that you know in regard to the accused in New York, are the facts sworn to by Thomas, who arrested him—that he was in disguise, that he gave a false name, and that he made divers untrue statements in regard to himself; then is his character as a spy still more strongly proved, according to Mr. Brady, because he is here, a rebel officer, in disguise, practising deception, and without any assigned pretext or excuse.

Are these two facts and the legal conclusion therefrom, met by any explanation, by any rebutting testimony?

Has any evidence been offered to change this fatal *prima facies* of the case?

The accused came to Ohio, says Mr. Brady, to perform a belligerent act. Unfortunately there is no such proof.

He *might*, says Mr. Brady, have come to Ohio and to New York on some innocent errand, or some errand of humanity. He *might*, indeed. But where is the proof that he *did?*

Has he purged himself of his criminality as a spy in Ohio or New York? Has he, in the language of the authorities which I have read, returned to the belligerent army, or to the navy in which he holds rank, and been captured in battle?

This is not even claimed or argued. He *did* go back to Canada, whose neutral rights he had violated, in September. He *did* attempt to go back to Canada in December. But he did not return to the insurgent States, nor was he taken prisoner in lawful or honorable warfare.

Now, Mr. President and gentlemen of the Commission, I do *not* ask you to set aside, but I *do* ask you not to enlarge or to disregard the narrow limits of that rule of law which discharges from guilt a spy who, having returned to the field of legitimate warfare, has been captured on the field of battle.

This rule is arbitrary. It is an exception to the general rule of civilized war, which inflicts ignominious death on all who violate its humane regulations by acts of perfidy, baseness, and treacherous hostility. It is your duty to see that this exception is not enlarged.

II. I now proceed, may it please the Court, to the inquiry as to the law and the evidence in support of specifications 1st, 2d, and 6th, under Charge I. As matter of law, do the facts alleged in these specifications constitute violations of the laws of civilized warfare, and, as matter of fact, are those allegations proved?

I shall not spend much time in answering what was so ingeniously argued by the learned counsel in regard to the legal meaning of the word *guerrilla*. That word occurs only in the 6th specification, and is there quite immaterial—mere surplusage—and might be stricken out and leave that specification as complete as are the 1st and 2d specifications.

I might admit, for the purpose of argument, that if the word guerrilla had now, and in our service, the same signification which belonged to it at the time when Gen. Halleck published, in San Francisco, his work on International Law, there would be weight as well as ingenuity in Mr. Brady's argument; though even then I should ask you merely to omit the word in your finding of guilty on the 6th specification. But, as the Judge Advocate General (*Digest*, p. 66) informs us, this word guerrilla, during this unhappy war, has acquired a peculiar and well-settled meaning, so that it is as idle to go back to Gen. Halleck, or the old dictionaries or treatises, for its present significancy, as it would be to go back to Cicero for the laws of modern warfare.

If the evidence in this case shows that the accused engaged in hostile acts which are forbidden by the law of war, you may call him brigand or raider, guerrilla or guerrillero, prowler or robber, he is still amenable to this Court, whatever may have been said by writers of a former and less civilized period. We do not go back to Cicero, nor even so far as Pufendorf, Bynkershoeck, or Grotius, to discover precisely what is now the law of war. We may go back to our Divine Master and His teachings in Judea, to discover the pure fountains of that law of love which has now found its way into the very code of war, and we may thence follow downward to our own day the course of Christianity in its influence upon Government, social institutions, and rules of civil conduct, and at last discover what are to-day the rules of civilized warfare. And in that code, as it now exists, we shall learn that warriors are not allowed to lay aside their uniforms, and the badges of their profession, to assume the disguise of peaceful citizens, to creep insidiously into the midst of peaceful and unsuspicious communities, and assassinate leading individuals, set fire at night to crowded theatres and hotels, or lay obstructions across railroads, and hurl men, women, and children indiscriminately to destruction; and that for atrocities and infamous attempts of this description, no command, no commission, no public manifesto, can be pleaded or proved in justification, extenuation, or mitigation.

President Woolsey, in his *Introduction to the Study of International Law* (2d Ed., p. 214) observes, that among the rules which lie at the basis of a humane system of war, is the rule that "war is waged between Governments by persons whom they authorize, and is not waged *against the passive inhabitants of a country.*"

And, as he says, the reasons why "guerrilla parties do not enjoy the full benefit of the laws of war, are, that they are annoying and insidious, that they put on and off with ease the character of a soldier, and that they are prone themselves to treat their enemies who fall into their hands with great severity."

In the enunciation of these humane doctrines all the recent text writers on public law are in harmony. But there is no work in existence devoted specially to the subject of irregular warfare, except the little treatise of Dr. Lieber, from which I have already quoted in speaking on the subject of spies, and from which I beg leave now to read a few passages that bear upon this second branch of the case on trial:

"There are cases in which the absence of a uniform may be taken as very serious *primâ facie* evidence against an armed prowler or marauder." * * * * "It makes a great difference whether the absence of uniform is used for the purpose of concealment or disguise in order to get by stealth within the lines of the invader for the destruction of life or property, or for pillage"— * * * * " nor can it be maintained in good faith, or with any respect for sound sense and judgment, that an individual—an armed prowler—shall be entitled to the protection of the laws of war— * * because his government or chief has issued a proclamation by which he calls upon the people to infest the bushes and commit homicides which every civilized nation will consider murders." (Pp. 16, 17.)

"The armed prowler is a simple assassin, and will thus always be considered by soldiers and citizens." (P. 20.)

"Armed bands that rise in the rear of an army are universally considered, if captured, brigands, and not prisoners of war. They unite the fourfold character of the spy, the brigand, the assassin, and the rebel, and cannot expect to be treated as a fair enemy of the regular war." (Pp. 20, 21.)

"No army, no society, engaged in war— * * can allow unpunished assassination, robbery, and devastation, without the deepest injury to itself, and disastrous consequences, which might change the very issue of the war." (P. 22.)

I have received from Dr. Lieber, and now propose to read as an authoritative exposition of the law which is to control this part of the case, a letter addressed to myself, and bearing date New York, February 5th, 1865:

"DEAR SIR: There is no work which treats in a clear and full manner like a law book, on spies, and so-called guerrillas, nor on the law and usages of war in general. In no war previous to our present one have these subjects received that minute and candid attention which we give them, although this is a war of a lawful government with insurgents.

"Nowhere have the spy and guerrilla been treated of more distinctly than in my pamphlet on 'Guerrilla Parties,' which the Government printed, and of which I would send you a copy had I one, and also of General Orders No. 100 (year 1863). I must say, however, that in my interleaved copy of this order I have added to § 88 'Enemies found in disguise or concealed, or lurking near the army, are by these facts deemed to be spies except they can prove that they are prisoners of war in the act of escaping.'

"I should certainly propose to add this were I consulted as to a new edition.

"I ought also to have given something on *enemies who in disguise come from the territory of a neutral to commit robbery or murder*, and those who may come from such territory in uniform.

"*I don't believe that such people, now called by the unacceptable term* RAIDERS, *have ever been treated of by any writer.*

"The thing created no doubt in the mind of any one. *They have always been treated as brigands, and it can easily be shown upon principle that they cannot be treated otherwise.*

"*Never*, so long as men have warred with one another—and that is pretty much as long as there have existed sufficient numbers to do so—has any belligerent been insolent enough to claim the protection of the laws of war for banditti who take passage on board a vessel, and then rise upon the captain and crew, or who gather in the territory of a friendly person, steal in disguise into the country of their enemy, and there commit murder or robbery. The insolence—I use the term now in a scientific meaning—the absurdity, and reckless disregard of honor, which characterize this proceeding, fairly stagger a jurist or a student of history. * * *.

"Your obedient servant,   FRANCIS LIEBER."

This, gentlemen of the Commission, is the voice of the law speaking from the lips of the living jurist—of that learned and eminent jurisconsult whom our Government, in the beginning of 1863, saw fit, first to consult and then to employ in drafting that manual of "Instructions for the Government of Armies of the United States in the Field," which, having been "approved by the President," became the will of the War Department, and was published as that "General Order No. 100," from which I have already quoted in the course of my argument.

With one reference to that order, from which I now read paragraph 101, I will close my citation of the authorities which determine the law applicable to the case now on trial:

"101. While deception in war is admitted as a just and necessary means of hostility, and is consistent with honorable warfare, the common law of war allows even capital punishment for clandestine or treacherous attempts to injure an enemy, because they are so dangerous, and it is so difficult to guard against them."

Reference was made by the counsel for the accused to the trials in

New York and Philadelphia, upon the charge of piracy, of certain rebel privateersmen. Let me remind this Court, that in those cases the civil judge, as matter of law, determined that the parties thus tried, though sheltered by a rebel commission, were pirates. It was executive policy, and not the law, which led to their exchange as prisoners of war.

The case of the steamer *Caroline* and the Canadian McLeod, to which Mr. Brady has alluded, can shed no light upon the present trial. England and the United States were friendly, not belligerent powers, and those border difficulties were adjusted without recourse to the laws of war.

And now, Mr. President, I come to the final inquiry in this most interesting and important trial. What are the facts proved by the evidence under the 1st, 2d, and 6th Specifications of Charge 1st?

I submit to the Court that we have proved,

1st. That the accused was and is a rebel officer.

2d. That he was within our lines in disguise.

3d. That he, at Kelly's Island, in Ohio, in September last, with the help of other rebel officers and soldiers in disguise, seized the American private steamboat *Philo Parsons*.

4th. That he stole the money and destroyed the freight on board of her.

5th. That in September, at Middle Bass Island, in Ohio, he, still in disguise, and with the same friends in disguise, seized in like manner another steamboat, the *Island Queen*, and scuttled and sunk her.

6th. That in December he came from Canada to Buffalo, in New York, in disguise, and with other disguised rebel officers and soldiers attempted unsuccessfully to throw a railroad train from the track.

7th. That he went back to Canada, and again returned in the same treacherous manner as before, and repeated his infamous attempt upon a night train from Dunkirk, and was caught as he fled from the scene of his unenviable exploits.

The evidence upon these points is not contradicted, and admits of no denial or doubt. I respectfully submit to the Court that the acts thus proved, having been done within our lines by rebel enemies in disguise, upon the persons and property of peaceable, unoffending, unsuspicious citizens, are acts of irregular warfare—call them raiding, brigandage, robbery, theft, piracy, plunder, murder, or assassination—are offences against the laws of God and the laws of man, against municipal law and the laws of war, and may be tried and punished by either municipal courts of civil jurisdiction, by court-martial, or by military commission. They are brought before you for trial. Yours is a rightful jurisdiction.

Upon you devolves the solemn duty of determining the issues in this case, which, to the accused, are the dread issues of life and death.

I have felt, Mr. President and gentlemen, oppressed, as I know you all must feel, with the terrible responsibility imposed upon me, and upon you, by the facts and the law in this case. But it is not a matter in which the dread of responsibility must be allowed to influence either your action or mine. It is important that you and I, sir, and our wives and children—that all of our fellow-citizens, may feel when they enter a railroad car within the loyal States that they are safe from all perils but those of ordinary travel; and that if any party of rebel soldiers in disguise, enemies of the Republic and friends of the Confederacy, attempt to place obstructions on the track, and throw off the train, they will be punished with the most exemplary speed, certainty, and severity. Enormities like this cannot be justified or screened from legal vengeance by the plea or proof of a military commission, command, or ratification, no matter how exalted may be the rank of the commander; since the law of war, which forbids and punishes the crime, is obligatory upon all.

It must have been apparent to you, gentlemen of the Commission, that in the conduct of the defence the accused was utterly embarrassed, perplexed, and at a loss to know how to protect himself; and that he was compelled to resort to two distinct, incongruous, and contradictory lines of defence: at one time seeking to escape from the jurisdiction of this Court by treating his acts as mere civil offences; and at another time claiming the protection of the laws of war as a legitimate and regular belligerent, acting in obedience to the lawful commands of his superior officers. Neither of these lines of defence, I respectfully submit, can stand for one moment against the charge and pressure of the law and the facts.

The accused, knowing the terrible risk he assumed, knowing the peril under which he acted, entered upon a scheme of illegal warfare upon the lake and upon the land. Some one on board the captured steamers uttered the foolish assertion, that with the stolen boats they meant to capture the U. S. armed steamer *Michigan*. Every movement of those captured boats proves the falsehood of that pretence. Not one single mile, not a rod, not an inch, did either of those vessels move under rebel direction toward that ship of war.

An act of lawful war! Seizing two passenger steamers, robbing the clerk, throwing overboard the freight, committing the crimes of pirates and of thieves, and not moving one barley corn of distance toward what is pretended to be the object and end of their warlike enterprise! Such a case does not admit of argument.

And so in regard to the defence of that scandalous attempt upon the train—that it was a simple attempt at robbery, and a mere civil offence, on the part of this " *humane and conscientious*" prisoner and his worthy associates, who with a force of five men, armed with five revolvers, a sledge-hammer, and a cold chisel, expected to capture a train of fifteen cars and fifteen hundred passengers, and to plunder the express-man's iron safe! It is a glaring absurdity. Why, sir, the moment the train halted and they saw the approach of three or four lanterns, this squad of express robbers jumped into their sleigh and fled for the Canada border!

All the evidence in this case, may it please the Court, tends to show that the accused was part and parcel of a wide-spread scheme of unlawful and irregular warfare along our whole Canadian line; whose purpose was, in any way and in every way, except by open and honorable hostility, to endanger the lives, destroy the property, and weaken the strength of those Yankee citizens whom these brigands of the border so bitterly hate.

The piracy of the lake, and the outrage on the railroad, were parts of that system of irregular warfare, under the fear of which no man, woman, or child can sleep with any feeling of security in our midst. Such atrocities are attempts, on the part of the rebel officers and soldiers who engage in and countenance them, to bring back war to its old condition of barbarism—to imitate the stealthy cruelty of the North American savage, who creeps under cover of midnight upon his unsuspecting victim, and smites him to death ere the sound of approaching footsteps has roused that victim from slumber. With the accused this savage purpose takes form in the robbery of steamboats and the destruction of railroad trains and travellers. In other hands, it manifests itself in midnight attempts to burn great cities. There is nothing of Christian civilization, nothing of regular warfare, nothing of a high, noble, bold, manly, chivalrous character about it. It is an outbreak of passions so bad and violent that they have overcome all the native elements of manliness, and have led men, of whom four years ago to have suspected such things possible would have been a calumny and a crime, to indulge in atrocities from month to month and year to year, such as have not stained the pages of warfare for two hundred years. And you sit here to-day, and I stand here to-day, as the representatives of recognized law and honorable warfare, to see that such outrages, when they are clearly and distinctly brought home to the guilty party by the evidence adduced upon the trial, shall not escape unpunished.

These proceedings having been submitted to Major Gen. John A. Dix, the Major General in command of the Department, he indorsed thereon his approval, and issued the following order:

The order of Maj. Gen. Dix upon this case is as follows:

GENERAL ORDERS }
No. 14. }   Headquarters Department of the East, }
New York City, *Feb.* 14*th*, 1865. }

I. Before a Military Commission which convened at Fort Lafayette, New York Harbor, by virtue of Special Orders No. 14, current series from these headquarters, of January 17, 1865, and of which Brigadier General FITZ HENRY WARREN, United States Volunteers, is president, was arraigned and tried JOHN Y. BEALL.

*   *   *   *   *   *

[Here follow the charges and specifications, and the finding of sentence.]

II. In reviewing the proceedings of the Commission, the circumstances on which the charges are founded, and the questions of law raised on the trial, the Major General commanding has given the most earnest and careful consideration to them all. The testimony shows that the accused, while holding a commission from the authorities at Richmond as Acting Master in the navy of the insurgent States, embarked at Sandwich, Canada, on board the *Philo Parsons*, an unarmed steamer, while on one of her regular trips, carrying passengers and freight from Detroit, in the State of Michigan, to Sandusky, in the State of Ohio. The Captain had been induced by Burley, one of the confederates of the accused, to land at Sandwich, which was not one of the regular stopping-places of the steamer, for the purpose of receiving them. Here the accused and two others took passage. At Malden, another Canadian port, and one of the regular stopping-places, about twenty-five more came on board. The accused was in citizen's dress, showing no insignia of his rank or profession, embarking as an ordinary passenger, and representing himself to be on a pleasure trip to Kelly's Island, in Lake Erie, within the jurisdiction of the State of Ohio.

After eight hours, he and his associates, arming themselves with revolvers and hand-axes, brought surreptitiously on board, rose on the crew, took possession of the steamer, threw overboard part of the freight, and robbed the clerk of the money in his charge, putting all on board under duress. Later in the evening he and his party took possession of another unarmed steamer (the *Island Queen*), scuttled her, and sent her adrift on the lake. These transactions occurred within the jurisdiction of the State of Ohio, on the 19th day of September, 1864.

On the 16th day of December, 1865, the accused was arrested near the Suspension Bridge, over the Niagara River, within the State of New York. The testimony shows that he and two officers of the insurgent States, Colonel Martin and Lieutenant Headley, with two other confederates, had made an unsuccessful attempt, under the direction of the first-named officer, to throw the passenger train coming from the West to Buffalo off the railroad track, for the purpose of robbing the express company. It is further shown that this was the third attempt in which the accused was concerned to accomplish the same object; that between two of these attempts the party, including the accused, went to Canada and returned, and that they were on their way back to Canada when he was arrested. In these transactions, as in that on Lake Erie, the accused, though holding a commission from the insurgent authorities at Richmond, was in disguise, procuring information, with the intention of using it, as he subsequently did, to inflict injury upon unarmed citizens of the United States and their private property. The substance of the charges against the accused is, that he was acting as a spy, and carrying on irregular or guerrilla warfare against the United States; in other words, he was acting in the twofold character of a spy and a guerrillero. He was found guilty on both charges, and sentenced to death; and the Major General commanding fully concurs in the judgment of the Commission. In all the transactions with which he was implicated—in one as a chief, and in the others as a subordinate agent—he was not only acting the part of a spy, in procuring information to be used for hostile purposes, but he was also committing acts condemned by the common judgment and the common conscience of all civilized States, except when done in open warfare by avowed enemies. Throughout these transactions, he was not only in disguise, but personating a false character. It is not at all essential to the purpose of sustaining the finding of the Commission, and yet it is not inappropriate to state, as an indication of the *animus* of the accused and his confederates, that the attempts to throw the railroad train off the track were made at night, when the obstruction would be less likely than in the daytime to be noticed by the engineer or conductor, thus putting in peril the lives of hundreds of men, women, and children. In these attempts three officers holding commissions in the military service of the insurgent States were concerned. The accused is shown by the testimony to be a man of education and refinement, and it is difficult to account for his agency in transactions so abhorrent to the moral sense, and so inconsistent with all the rules of honorable warfare.

The accused, in justification of the transaction on Lake Erie, produced the manifesto of Jefferson Davis, assuming the responsibility of the act, and declaring that it was done by his authority. It is hardly necessary to say that no such assumption can sanction an act not warranted by the laws of civilized warfare. If Mr. Davis were at the head of an independent government, recognized as such by other nations, he would have no power to sanction what the usages of civilized states have condemned. The Government of the United States, from a desire to mitigate the asperities of war, has given to the insurgents of the South the benefit of the rules which govern sovereign States in the conduct of hostilities with each other; and any violation of those rules should, for the sake of good order here, and the cause of humanity throughout the world, be visited with the severest penalty. War, under its mildest aspects, is the heaviest calamity that can befall our race; and he who, in a spirit of revenge, or with lawless violence, transcends the limits to which it is restricted by the common behest of all Christian communities, should receive the punishment which the common voice has declared to be due to the crime. The Major General commanding feels that a want of firmness and inflexibility, on his part, in executing the sentence of death in such a case, would be an offence against the outraged civilization and humanity of the age.

It is hereby ordered that the accused, JOHN Y. BEALL, be hanged by the neck till he is dead, on Governor's Island, on Saturday, the 18th day of February, inst., between the hours of 12 and 2 in the afternoon.

The commanding officer at Fort Columbus is charged with the execution of this order.

By command of Major Gen. DIX.

D. T. VAN BUREN, Col. A. A. G.

On the 17th February the execution of the sentence against Beall was suspended by the following order, viz.:

Headquarters Department of the East,
New York City, *Feb. 17th,* 1865.

Commanding Officer Fort Columbus,
New York Harbor.

You will suspend the execution of the sentence of John Y. Beall until further orders.

By command of Major General DIX,

(Signed)   D. T. VAN BUREN,

Colonel and Assistant Adjutant General.

On the same day an order was issued reconvening the Commission. This order, and the proceedings of the Commission in obedience thereto, appear from the following record:

Headquarters Department of the East,
New York City, *Feb. 20th*, 1865, 11 o'clock A. M.

The Commission appointed by Special Orders No. 14, par. 6, from these Headquarters, dated Jan. 17, 1865, reassembled in obedience to the following order:

SPECIAL ORDERS
No. 42.

Headquarters Department of the East,
New York City, *February 17th*, 1865.

1. The Military Commission of which Brigadier General Fitz Henry Warren, U. S. Vols., is President, and which was convened pursuant to Special Orders No. 14, current series from these Headquarters, N. Y. City, will reassemble at these Headquarters to-morrow at 10 o'clock A. M., or as soon hereafter as practicable, for the purpose of reconsideration of the finding in the case of *John Y. Beall*, for reasons more particularly set forth in communication herewith enclosed from the Major General Commanding the Department.

By command of Major General DIX,
(Signed)   D. T. VAN BUREN,
Assistant Adjutant General.

Present, all the members of the Commission, viz.:

Brig. General FITZ HENRY WARREN, U. S. V.
Brig. General W. H. MORRIS, U. S. V.
Colonel M. S. HOWE, 3d U. S. Cav.
Colonel H. DAY, U. S. Army.
Brev. Lieut. Col. R. F. O'BIERNE, 14th U. S. Infantry.
Major G. W. WALLACE, 6th U. S. Infantry.

Present, also, the Judge Advocate. The Commission was cleared for deliberation.

The foregoing order was read aloud by the Judge Advocate.

The President then read the following communication from the Major General Commanding:

Headquarters Department of the East,
New York City, *February 18th*, 1865.

GENERAL: I have suspended the order for the execution of John Y. Beall, and have reconvened your Military Commission, that I might send the proceedings in that case back to the Commission for a revision of the findings therein.

I would particularly call the attention of the Commission to the finding upon the 3d Specification under Charge 2d.

A familiar rule of law requires that the finding should meet, and affirm or deny, every averment in the Specification. This is not done by the present finding, except by implication. The finding negatives the averment of date, and omits all mention of the other averments, leaving it to be inferred that the Commission considered the Specification sustained by the proof in every other particular. If such were the opinion of the Commission, the rule of law to which I have referred would be complied with by finding the accused "Guilty, omitting the word September, and substituting the word December;" or, "Not Guilty as to the day averred, but guilty of acting as a spy, at or near Suspension Bridge, in the State of New York, on or about December 16, 1864."

The Commission may deem it well to consider and determine once more whether the proof under Specifications 1 and 2, charge 2d, establishes the characteristics of a spy, viz., an enemy clandestinely within our lines to obtain information to be used for hostile purposes.

I do not make this last suggestion for the purpose of raising a doubt in regard to the correctness of the finding, but that the judgment of the Commission may be placed beyond all question.

I am, very respectfully, yours,

JOHN A. DIX,
Major General.

Brig. General FITZ HENRY WARREN,
President Military Commission.

The Commission then reopened the case of John Y. Beall, and reconsidered the finding upon Specification 3d under Charge 2d.

Upon careful consideration of the evidence recorded in the proceedings, the Commission find the accused, John Y. Beall, of Specification 3d under Charge 2d not guilty as to the day averred, but guilty of acting as a spy at or near Suspension Bridge, in the State of New York, on or about Dec. 16, 1864.

After careful deliberation the Commission find no reason to reconsider their finding on either Charge, or any other Specification, and do therefore reaffirm their sentence, two-thirds of the members of the Commission concurring therein.

(Signed) FITZ HENRY WARREN,
Brigadier General U. S. Volunteers, President.

JOHN A. BOLLES,
  Major and Aide-de-camp,
    Judge Advocate.

These Proceedings were laid before the Major General commanding, who endorsed thereon the following approval and order, on the 21st of February, Tuesday:

The proceedings, finding, and sentence are approved, and the accused, John Y. Beall, will be hanged by the neck till he is dead, on Governor's Island, on Friday, the 24th day of February, 1865. The commanding officer at Fort Columbus is charged with the execution of this order.

(Signed)   JOHN A. DIX,
Major General Commanding.

Any of these Books sent free by mail to any address on receipt of Price.

RECENT PUBLICATIONS
OF
D. APPLETON & COMPANY,
443 & 445 BROADWAY, NEW YORK.

Life and Correspondence of Theodore

PARKER, Minister of the Twenty-eighth Congregational Society, Boston. By JOHN WEISS. With two Portraits on Steel, fac-simile of Handwriting, and nineteen Wood Engravings. 2 vols., 8vo. 1,008 pages.

"These volumes contain an account of Mr. Parker's childhood and self-education; of the development of his theological ideas; of his scholarly and philosophical pursuits; and of his relation to the Anti-Slavery cause, and to the epoch in America which preceded the civil war. His two visits to Europe are described in letters and extracts from his journal. An autobiographical fragment is introduced in relation to Mr. Parker's early life, and his letters of friendship on literary, speculative, and political topics, are freely interspersed. The illustrations represent scenes connected with various periods of Mr. Parker's life, the houses he dwelt in, his country haunts, the meeting house, his library, and the Music Hall in which he preached."

Catechism of the Steam Engine,

In its various Applications to Mines, Mills, Steam Navigation, Railways, and Agriculture. With Practical Instructions for the Manufacture and Management of Engines of every Class. By JOHN BOURNE, C. E. New and Revised Edition. 1 vol., 12mo. Illustrated.

'In offering to the American public a reprint of a work on the Steam Engine so deservedly successful, and so long considered standard, the Publishers have not thought it necessary that it should be an exact copy of the English edition. There were some details in which they thought it could be improved and better adapted to the use of American Engineers. On this account, the size of the page has been increased to a full 12mo, to admit of larger illustrations, which, in the English edition, are often on too small a scale; and some of the illustrations themselves have been supplied by others equally applicable, more recent, and to us more familiar examples. The first part of Chapter XL., devoted in the English edition to English portable and fixed agricultural engines, in this edition gives place entirely to illustrations from American practice, of steam engines as applied to different purposes, and of appliances and machines necessary to them. But with the exception of some of the illustrations and the description of them, and the correction of a few typographical errors, this edition is a faithful transcript of the latest English edition."

Life of Edward Livingston,

Mayor of the City of New York; Member of Congress; Senator of the United States; Secretary of State; Minister to France; Author of a System of Penal Law for Louisiana; Member of the Institute of France, etc. By CHARLES H. HUNT, with an Introduction by GEORGE BANCROFT. 1 vol., 8vo.

"One of the purest of statesmen and the most genial of men, was Edward Livingston, whose career is presented in this volume. * * * *

"The author of this volume has done the country a service. He has given us in a becoming form an appropriate memorial of one whom succeeding generations will be proud to name as an American jurist and statesman."—*Evangelist.*

D. APPLETON & CO.'S PUBLICATIONS.

History of the Romans under the
Empire. By CHARLES MERIVALE, B. D., late Fellow of St. John's College. 7 vols., small 8vo. Handsomely printed on tinted paper.

CONTENTS:

Vols. I. and II.—Comprising the History to the Fall of Julius Cæsar.
Vol. III.—To the Establishment of the Monarchy by Augustus.
Vols. IV. and V.—From Augustus to Claudius, B. C. 27 to A. D. 54.
Vol. VI.—From the Reign of Nero, A. D. 54, to the Fall of Jerusalem, A. D. 70.
Vol. VII.—From the Destruction of Jerusalem, A. D. 70, to the Death of M. Aurelius.

This valuable work terminates at the point where the narrative of Gibbon commences.

. . . "When we enter on a more searching criticism of the two writers, it must be admitted that Merivale has as firm a grasp of his subject as Gibbon, and that his work is characterized by a greater freedom from prejudice, and a sounder philosophy.

. . . "This History must always stand as a splendid monument of his learning, his candor, and his vigorous grasp of intellect. Though he is in some respects inferior to Macaulay and Grote, he must still be classed with them, as one of the second great triumvirate of English historians."—*North American Review, April*, 1863.

Thirty Poems.
By WM. CULLEN BRYANT, 1 volume, 12mo.

"No English poet surpasses him in knowledge of nature, and but few are his equals. He is better than Cowper and Thomson in their special walks of poetry, and the equal of Wadsworth, that great high priest of nature."—*The World.*

Hints to Riflemen.
By H. W. S. CLEVELAND. 1 vol., 12mo. Illustrated with numerous Designs of Rifles and Rifle Practice.

"I offer these hints as the contribution of an old sportsman, and if I succeed in any degree in exciting an interest in the subject, my end will be accomplished, even if the future investigations of those who are thus attracted should prove any of my opinions to be erroneous."—*Extract from Preface.*

Queen Mab.
A new Novel. By JULIA KAVANAGH. 1 vol., 12mo.

"No English novelist of the present day ought to hold, we think, a higher rank in her own peculiar walk of literature than Miss Kavanagh. There is a freshness of originality about all her works, and an individual character stamped on each,—there is, moreover, a unity of thought and feeling, a harmony, so to speak, pervading each separate work, that plainly speaks original genius, while the womanly grace of her etchings of character, is a marvel of artistic excellence."—*Tablet.*

My Cave Life in Vicksburg.
By a Lady. 1 vol., 12mo.

"Altogether we commend the book as worth more than almost any dozen of books on the war we have lately noticed."

attention from the more quiet and influential working of science and art, social progress and individual thought,—the living seed sown, and the fruit borne, in the field broken up by those outward changes.

While special care will be bestowed on those periods and nations, the history of which is scarcely to be found in any works accessible to the general reader, the more familiar parts of history will be treated in their due proportion to the whole work. It will be found, we trust, by no means the least valuable part of the scheme,—that the portions of history which are generally looked at by themselves,—those, for example, of Greece and Rome, and of our own country,—will be regarded from a common point of view with all the rest: a view which may, in some cases, modify the conclusions drawn by classical partiality and national pride.

The spirit of the work,—at least if the execution be true to the conception,—will be equally removed from narrow partisanship and affected indifference. The historian, as well as the poet, must be in earnest,

> "Dower'd with the hate of hate, the scorn of scorn,
> The love of love;"

but he must also be able to look beyond the errors, and even the virtues, of his fellow-men, to the great ends which the Supreme Ruler of events works out by their agency:—

> "Yet I doubt not through the ages one increasing purpose runs,
> And the thoughts of men are widen'd with the process of the suns."

No pains will be spared to make this history scholarlike in substance and popular in style. It will be founded on the best authorities, ancient and modern, original and secondary. The vast progress recently made in historical and critical investigations, the results obtained from the modern science of comparative philology, and the discoveries which have laid open new sources of information concerning the East, afford such facilities as to make the present a fit epoch for our undertaking.

The work will be divided into three Periods, each complete in itself, and will form Eight Volumes in Demy Octavo.

I.—ANCIENT HISTORY, Sacred and Secular; from the Creation to the Fall of the Western Empire, in A. D. 476. Two Volumes.

II.—MEDIEVAL HISTORY, Cival and Ecclesiastical; from the Fall of the Western Empire to the taking of Constantinople by the Turks, in A. D. 1453. Two Volumes.

III.—MODERN HISTORY; from the Fall of the Byzantine Empire to our own Times. Four Volumes.

It will be published in 8 vols., 8vo. Price in cloth $3 50 per vol. Sheep $4 50. Volume 1 now ready.

NEW YORK: D. APPLETON & CO., Publishers.

D. APPLETON & CO.'S PUBLICATIONS.

THE
NEW AMERICAN CYCLOPÆDIA.

EDITED BY

GEORGE RIPLEY AND CHARLES A. DANA.

PUBLISHED BY

D. APPLETON & COMPANY, NEW YORK.

In 16 Vols. 8vo, Double Columns, 750 pages each.

Price, *Cloth*, $5.00; *Sheep*, $6.00; *Half Morocco*, $6.50; *Half Russia*, $7.50 *per Vol.*

Every one that reads, every one that mingles in society, is constantly meeting with allusions to subjects on which he needs and desires further information. In conversation, in trade, in professional life, on the farm, in the family, practical questions are continually arising, which no man, well read or not, can always satisfactorily answer. If facilities for reference are at hand, they are consulted, and not only is the curiosity gratified, and the stock of knowledge increased, but perhaps information is gained and ideas are suggested that will directly contribute to the business success of the party concerned.

But how are these facilities for reference to be had? How are the million to procure a library? How can the working-man hope to bring within his reach the whole circle of sciences, and every point of human knowledge as developed up to the present moment? A good Cyclopædia is the only work which supplies this want.

With a Cyclopædia, embracing every conceivable subject, and having its topics alphabetically arranged, not a moment is lost. The matter in question is found at once, digested, condensed, stripped of all that is irrelevant and unnecessary, and verified by a comparison of the best authorities. Moreover, while only men of fortune can collect a library complete in all the departments of knowledge, a Cyclopædia, worth in itself for purposes of reference at least a thousand volumes, is within the reach of all,—the clerk, the merchant, the professional man, the farmer, the mechanic. In a country like ours, where the humblest may be called to responsible positions requiring intelligence and general information, the value of such a work cannot be overestimated.

www.ingramcontent.com/pod-product-compliance
Lightning Source LLC
Chambersburg PA
CBHW031123160426
43192CB00008B/1091